Altar'd

FAITH-BUILDING EVIDENCE
LEADING TO NEW LIFE

Jay Cavaiani

Altar'd

FAITH-BUILDING EVIDENCE
LEADING TO NEW LIFE

Jay Cavaiani

✝ Carpenter's Son Publishing

Altar'd FAITH-BUILDING EVIDENCE LEADING TO NEW LIFE

© 2015 by Jay Cavaiani

Scriptures taken from the The Holy Bible,
English Standard Version® (ESV®) unless otherwise indicated.
English Standard Version® (ESV®)
Copyright © 2001 by Crossway,
a publishing ministry of Good NewsPublishers.
All rights reserved. ESV Text Edition: 2007

Published by Carpenter Son Publishing, Franklin, Tennessee
Edited by Robert Irvin
Cover Design by Suzanne Lawing
Interior Layout Design by Debbie Manning Sheppard
Printed in the United States of America
978-1-942587-10-1

One of the hopes of **Altar'd** is that it would be used by
Christians and churches as an outreach tool
for seekers and current unbelievers.

You may go to **altardthebook.com**
to order in bulk for this reason or to order books
for your small group use.

This greeting page is designed to be used by individuals and
churches to attach (glue or stick) your church information
over mine below. In this way the book can be used to both
encourage people to faith and invite them to church.
*Blessings to you all in your ministry to people
for the sake of Jesus and His Kingdom.*

Jay Cavaiani

You're invited to visit Brandybrook!

PASTOR, BRANDYBROOK CHRISTIAN CHURCH
www.brandybrookchurch.org
Wales, Wisconsin

Contents

Dedication

To all my friends who I have
shared with through the years:
this is for you.

Dan, Greg, Tim, Brad, Bob, Dave, Steve, and Todd
from the Wisconsin/Colorado Cup:
this is making good on my promise.

Tom, Jasmine, Beau, Mike, Matt, Dave, John,
Joe, Scott, and Bob from Nag Men's Club:
you were in my thoughts as I wrote this book.

Bicycle Joe, the same goes for you.

To all my extended family:
I hope the evidence in the book
encourages you in faith.

Prelude

Do you believe Jesus Christ is the Savior of the world?

If so, why? If not, why not?

What does it mean that Jesus Christ is said to be a Savior, and why does anyone even need a Savior?

This book was written to help people gain confidence, through faith-building evidence, that Jesus is the Lamb of God who takes away the sins of the world. **Altar'd** will help display the reliability of the Bible, and as a result, the incredible message of purpose and eternal life it contains can be trusted.

It has been said that sometimes we choose our books and sometimes our books choose us. However it is that you came into contact with this book, my hope is that God uses it to fan your faith into flame and infuse your life with greater purpose in serving His Kingdom.

Why Did This Book Come to Be?

In the early to mid-1990s I did not understand why I was taking up air on planet earth. The question I wrestled with was this: Why do I exist? That truly is a great question for all of us. At that point in my life I did not have a lasting purpose. I also wondered what would happen to me when I died. I did not know if God existed, and if He did, I surely did not know much about Him. With curiosity sparked by some people around me, I started by reading the Bible and then began visiting a nondenominational Bible church. Not long after, my life was dramatically transformed. In chapter 3 of this book I share the story about how God transformed my life.

When I first became a believer, at times I would doubt. I believed, but I did not know why I believed. Having doubt bothered me greatly, and it drove me to discover why I believed. I began as a young believer learning evidence that helped me believe more fully. As I learned the evidence, any time doubt would come, I would recite to myself the reasons I believed. Pretty soon, doubt was defeated.

For the past twenty years I have researched a great deal and have come to a clear understanding of many powerful evidences that have helped me and others believe. Knowing how great it has been to gain this confidence, I deeply long that the people whom I love would also discover this convincing evidence. My great hope is that they would receive the positive life change and purpose that God brings through believing.

Through golf and other common interests, I have had the opportunity to share with many people whom I care about. I have tried to learn how to condense examples of evidence so that when I have a chance to share with them, I can give them something that may prompt them to seek as I did. There is a great difficulty that exists in this scenario. In order for the evidence to truly make sense, one must understand the history and story of God to see how God has fulfilled and followed through on His Word. Many powerful evidences exist, that have the ability to shine a bright light of faith, proofs strong enough to penetrate the soul of our minds—but they take more than a brief conversation to be fully discerned.

One day, already beginning to feel led by God to write a book, I proposed the following question to a group of friends. "If I wrote a book sharing why I believe, would you read it?" They said that they would. Ever since, I have been committed to writing it for them. To me, this book is making good on a promise. I did not really know all that I was committing to. It definitely has become a much bigger (and more expensive) project than I anticipated. It may sound cliché, but I mean it from the bottom of my heart: if one person responds in faith, it is all worth it. The value of a human life receiving the gift of eternal life is immeasurable. My great hope is that many people will receive eternal life and, as a result, **"Altar"** their lives to live for the one who first **Altar'd** his.

Altar'd follows the dramatic story of God and His use of a sacrificial offering, throughout history, to restore His relationship with the masterpiece of His creation: you and me. **Altar'd** illustrates powerful evidence in order to help people believe and ultimately offer their lives to be used by God.

One more important note: My greatest hope is that this book will be given to all those whom we love to help them believe. Having everyone start at the beginning of the book and take in the full evidence would be my desire. However, the last chapter is a summary chapter which provides a more succinct display of the evidence contained in this book. That power-packed chapter is included so no one puts away this book without taking in the summary, titled **Altar'd** at Once.

Blessings,

Jay

...and I pray that the sharing of your faith may become effective for the full knowledge of every good thing that is in us for the sake of Christ.

(PHILEMON 1:6, ESV)

Chapter One

Rescued

On a beautiful, warm summer day, a group of friends, on a weeklong vacation, are enjoying the Florida sun, beach, and warm southern ocean waters. The beach that day is filled with happy people relaxing on beach towels, while others are playing catch with their kids or smiling from ear to ear as they catch a wave on a boogie board close to shore. Ah yes, the free roller coaster of God that comes by every ten seconds. There are bright-red umbrellas up and down the shoreline and an occasional lifeguard post. However, today, there are no guards on duty.

On this hot summer day, with perfect water temperatures, there is a group of swimmers, or, shall we say, waders, who are attracted to some fellowship just outside the surf. They had tried swimming close to shore, but after the first couple of waves tumble them over a few times like a washing machine, they find it a bit more relaxing by venturing just beyond the cresting surf. After they finally push through the crashing waves, they get to a spot where they can relax and hold a conversation. Sometimes, however, these waves are not consistent, and a couple of them crest over farther from shore, taking our recreational swimmers under once again. So they decide to wade out just a bit farther until they reach a more peaceful spot. Ah, finally. Relaxation.

Eventually they hear someone from shore trying to get their attention. The swimmers mumble to each other, "What did they say?" One of the swimmers thinks he hears, "Come back in a little closer." These swimmers, who are Northerners, look at each other, shrug their shoulders, and comment to themselves, "Hey, we're fine; leave us alone." So they wave off those yelling to them. After all, they're having a great time. A little while later they get a little farther out, but not so much that it seems significant, and they vaguely—once again—hear someone calling from shore. They cannot hear what is being said, but they're pretty sure someone is saying that they should come in closer to shore. At the moment they are in the middle of a great conversation, so they agree, after they wrap it up, that they will begin their journey back to shore.

A while later, as the waders get a little sidetracked in their conversations, they look back to shore and, to their surprise, the umbrellas they saw lined up along the shore earlier now look like little dimples, and the people look like ants! Immediately, panic sets in; they are overwhelmed with anxiety. What these Northerners do not realize, and had missed on the local news that day, was that there was a rip current warning, which is both a very dangerous and yet common occurrence. A rip current is a strong flow of water heading away from shore and out to sea. The riptide develops when certain wind and weather conditions affect the flow of water outside the surf. Dangerously, this water moves out to sea much faster than one can swim. People die from these dangerous rip currents each year. The locals knew the danger, but those outside the region did not have the *knowledge* to realize they were in danger. They have now been perilously pulled out to sea. The reality is this:

these Northerners had been in danger the whole time, but did not know it! Because they did not possess the proper knowledge of the sea, they did not understand the warnings.

This group of swimmers also did not possess the local knowledge about what to do *after* being caught in a rip current. Perhaps what I share next will save someone's life. If you ever get caught in a rip current, you cannot beat it by swimming against it. No one can swim fast enough to overcome a rip current. You have to have the *knowledge*—counterintuitive to what it seems *should* be the case—to let it take you out to sea as you swim sideways, which will be, in fact, diagonally heading out to sea due to the flow of water. Many times, a rip current will not exist up and down the entire shoreline. There will be a flow of water like a river, but if you can get out of the flow, you have a chance to swim back in. If you don't have this knowledge, you will exhaust yourself swimming against the current—until you have nothing left. Unfortunately, without this valuable knowledge, these Northerners, in complete panic, desperately try to swim back to shore and thus place themselves directly in the path of the rip current. When they sense they are not making any progress and their strength has run out, they come to a very critical realization.

They cannot save themselves.
A rescuer is needed.

Finally, they have come to the correct realization. It is *then* that a person is ready to be rescued.

You may be thinking: *Jay, what are you talking about? What is the point of this story?* The point is that this story is about everyone, including me. This is an incredibly important understanding, which we all need. What God deeply wants us to know is that we need to be rescued, and that He has paid the price to rescue us. God desires that we would live a life that is grateful to Him, but before we can be filled with gratefulness we need to know why we are to be grateful! And here lies the problem. In order for those swimmers to be rescued, they needed first to *know* that they needed to be rescued. The people on shore, who had the local knowledge, tried to give them the warning, but without a proper understanding of the danger, and their need, they did not heed the warning message that could have saved them.

Many in the world today are caught in a rip current that is taking them away from God. They are living life "outside of the surf" and outside of the life that God desires for them. The problem is they don't realize they need the message from shore that would save them from the deadly current. With their lack of knowledge they may think they are good enough swimmers to save themselves.

The problem is the current is too strong. The reality is we all need a Savior.

Imagine for a moment...you have been caught in a rip current. You are out to sea, and your strength is running out. Hypothermia can set in, even in warm water temperatures, if you are in it long enough. Your muscles are not working well, and you are beginning to drown. You are desperate. You are about to give up. Your life is flashing before you. You are thinking of your spouse, family, and children. You are beginning to cry out and maybe, for one of the few times, pray. *"God, help me!!* . . . God, if you are there, will you help me! God, I want to live. I know I have not lived life the way you have wanted, but if you save me, if you will help me, I will give my life to serve you!" Here is *the* question of this book:

If God saved you, would you offer Him your life?

In brief, that is what it means to be **Altar'd** There are two audiences in mind for this book. First, it is for believers, to increase their confidence in the rescuer's message and, as a result, fully offer their lives to the one who rescued them. The second audience is all whom those believers deeply care about. Most people who do not yet believe are not going out to buy themselves a book to find faith. It is the responsibility of the believer to become an agent of rescue and follow their rescuer by sharing His message with all whom they care about.

Perhaps you received this book because someone cared about you enough that they purchased a copy and had the guts to give it to you. They likely know the ocean and already have realized they could never make it back to shore on their own strength, so they have raised their hand to the rescuer—and rescued He has. I am one of those people. I thought I was living the dream, but really, I was out to sea. Soon I will share with you my story. All I will tell you for now is that the greatest thing that ever happened to me was realizing I needed a rescuer, and through humbling myself to be rescued, I received a new, exciting, purposeful life.

The purpose of this book is to convince people there is a God who sent a Savior to rescue people who desperately need to be rescued. The hardest part about rescuing those outside the surf of God is helping them realize their need to be rescued. The beauty is that once a person discovers their need, and is rescued, they can and should become so impacted by the experience that it radically alters their reason for waking up each day and taking up air on planet earth. In short, their life becomes an offering to the One who has rescued them. They may even become a rescuer!

What has been said to this point is straightforward and perhaps even bold. This message, regarding our need to be rescued, comes from the Bible. So if the Bible is true, then the message also is true. So then, the strength of this message relies on the authenticity of the Bible. This then leads to a question: How can we know whether the Bible is true?

Questions for Discussion

1) What would you describe as the beliefs and habits in our culture that are pulling people away from God?

2) The waders did not think they needed help from those who had the local knowledge. How important is humility in recognizing our need for God and growing in faith in Him and why?

3) Please share with the group about your family, career, and story of faith at this point in your journey. With humility, simply share your faith history and where you are in terms of God and faith. This will help us understand one another better as we go through this journey together. It may be good to set a timer at five minutes per person and give each person a one-minute warning, or set an appropriate time given your group's needs and time frame.

4) In general, have each person respond to the essence of these questions: When it comes to the Bible, how would you summarize your current knowledge? What is the Bible to you? What have you been taught regarding the Bible's accuracy and truthfulness?

Chapter Two

Putting the Bible on Trial

Let's start with some basic questions.

How can one know if a God who rescues even exists?

There are many in the world today who are quite uncertain whether there is a God, and even if there is, they wonder whether there is a source of truth to accurately discover more about Him. In addition, very common today is a belief that it is up to each individual person to define what is their truth . . . versus there being a trusted source to guide us in truth. Some of the debated ideas today—abortion, gay marriage, pornography, the legalization of marijuana, and more—are often debated on what many believe is an equal playing field. The field of public opinion. If there is not a moral source that can be trusted, then it makes sense that all that remains is our personal opinions. So a very important question follows our first question.

Does God truly exist, and if He does, can the Bible be trusted to accurately contain His message?

For many, the conclusion is that the Bible is simply an interesting book with some good information, but ultimately, it cannot be trusted to accurately contain God's message for today. This common position could be described as follows: "Where I agree with the Bible, it has some good, even wise, advice. But where I do not agree, it probably needs to be updated. I mean, it is rather *old*, isn't it?"

Putting the Bible on trial

Let's say we are going to put the Bible on trial to see if it is true and can be trusted. The first step in such a trial would be finding a pool of jurors. Clearly, anyone stating that they had already made a prior determination that it was true, or that it was not, would be eliminated from the pool of potential jurors. Individuals who are undecided would be selected to be on that jury. My hope is that if you are currently undecided, that you will ultimately trust both that there is a God and that the Bible contains an accurate recording of His message. I hope that you commit to being in the jury pool for the entirety of the trial. But no matter what you do, please don't put this book away until you read "**Altar'd** at Once: The Summary Chapter" (found near the end of this book), which is a summation of the evidence presented. It is worth the wait, and I encourage you to stay the course. I've written that chapter to help anyone who can only make the closing arguments portion of this trial. In the full trial, evidence will be presented that will allow for a knowledgeable and convincing determination to be made. The mistake many make in our world today is reaching a determination prior to hearing the evidence. Isn't it simply logical to hear the evidence before making a judgment? Heaven, Hell, and the very purpose for our existence are all at stake. It is too important to not devote the time needed to examine the evidence. This next story may help illustrate the magnitude of the questions we're considering.

Have you ever imagined a world without God?

One day I was sitting in the bleachers of a district-wide track meet. I struck up a conversation with a mom with a son who shares the same class as my son. We briefly engaged in polite conversation. As we continued to chat, a door was opened to discuss things of God. It became clear during our discussion that this lovely woman did not attend church and was unsure about the existence of God. She shared her beliefs, and it became evident that they were not based on any particular source, but rather on those of her own personal opinion.

I remember asking her a question that day: Do you think life would be better without God? This question caught her off guard. She had to pause to think about it. Let's do that. Let's all venture down that path for a moment. If there is no God, then what? Well, to start, if there is no God then there is no Heaven and there is no eternal life. It means that when we are done here, it's over. Simply left to rot, six feet under, in a casket, and to never see the light again. I think we all have higher aspirations than becoming fertilizer. If there is no God, are we not just like the wild animals? Not created, but rather evolved—all from survival of the fittest. So then, just as animals do not have rules to live by, we too would have no moral code to live by. Does an animal do wrong when it takes the life of another?

Without a moral imperative, anarchy is all that exists. Anything goes. Let me ask it another way. Would the world be better as a place in which everyone simply decides what is *their* right, or *their* wrong, without any moral guidance to rely on? Where would that get us? If someone is bigger or stronger than I am and wants what I have and kills me and takes what I have, who is to say that is wrong? Is that not what a lion does when it wants a prey? After all, if there is no God, then we humans are just animals. A higher form of a beast, perhaps, but nonetheless a beast. No! This is not the world I want to raise my three children in. I believe there is a God who has provided a source to guide us. That source exists for us to learn for our own good what is right and wrong.

**However, my desire for a life where God is true
and there is guidance from His Word
does not make it true.**

Throughout this book I will be presenting the story of God and the grand purpose He has for our lives. In the process of sharing this story I will be providing evidence, strong evidence, which will display how we can know He exists, and that the Bible can be trusted.

But before starting our trial, why listen to me?

Questions for Discussion

1) Many people have disregarded the Bible without first reading it thoroughly and examining the evidence. Why do you think this is the case?

2) If God is true, then the blessings of believing are great, and the consequences of not believing are grave. This being the case, if you could advise someone on what would be a worthy investigation of whether God is true and whether He can be trusted, what advice would you give them?

3) Think deeply. What if God and the Bible did not exist? What do you think our world would be like? Is it possible that many have not recognized how much God and the Bible have shaped our world? How is the world a better place to raise your family because God and the Bible have shaped it?

4) Perhaps this book could be used in the life of someone you know for them to consider the evidence, or even to join your study. Perhaps each person could think about who that person might be in their life.

Chapter Three

Why Should You Listen to Me?

 B efore I proceed, I would like to let you in on my life and what God has done to shape this message. One of the most important aspects in trusting the message of a person is how you view their personal *ethos*. A person's ethos could be described as their character. Does this person really know what they are talking about, and does their life demonstrate what they believe? Simply put, do they practice what they preach? The greater the ethos, typically, the greater the believability. I hope after reading my story you will find me more believable.

I grew up with two amazing parents; they are still alive and happily married today. That fact alone means I am very blessed indeed. My parents raised their children as members of the Catholic Church and we were what I think anyone would consider a pretty typical suburban, fortunate, American family. We learned right from wrong and had a sense of morality; however, it was not what I would now call Christ-centered, but rather "cultural American." When I was in eighth grade, my parents were concerned I was becoming sexually active, and although they did not approve, they helped me learn about proper protection. I remember going to confession, a couple years later, now a sophomore in high school—and still a virgin, by the way—but now with a girlfriend. I told the priest that I was still a virgin, and I interpreted his response to me as something to the effect that I still had college ahead and that such a goal was going to be nearly impossible to maintain. I took it as "Good job, son, but you likely won't make it until marriage." So I figured that if I was not going to make it anyway, I might as well give up now and get started. It was not long, and I was no longer a virgin.

Through my junior year of high school we went to church most weeks and said a brief, rote prayer at dinnertime. Hey, at least we prayed. With that being said, I can only remember one time the Bible being opened in our home; however, I cannot remember the reason. Growing up, I liked sports, girls, and partying with friends. Around this time, my brother and I complained about going to church, and my parents, growing weary in forcing us, relented and said that we could now make our own choice. That was pretty much it for me going to church, besides perhaps Christmas and Easter with the family. I mean no lack of respect to my parents in sharing any part of my story. I cannot tell you how special, awesome, and loving my parents were, and are. At that time, however, they could not pass on to us what they did not yet fully know or understand. This leads to a very important statement.

One cannot give what they don't have.

If we do not have food we cannot give it. If we do not have a dime we cannot give one. In the same way, without a fullness of faith we cannot pass on what we do not yet have. Can you relate? Parents, my hope is that we gain more in our understanding and faith in God and, as a result, will have more to pass on to our children. God has the same desire.

In college, I got to the point that I doubted whether there was a God. I graduated in 1993 from the University of Wisconsin-Whitewater with a degree in psychology, primarily because that is what my dad's degree was in. I was a C student in high school, but when I got to college, despite the partying I was doing, I took my studies seriously and ended up graduating with honors. Immediately after graduation, I interviewed for a couple of jobs I did not obtain. Then, through a connection, I found myself interviewing for real estate positions. I had interviews with two different companies, and both wanted to hire me! I was pretty proud of that. After a few short months I discovered that if you have a pulse and claim to be motivated, you can get started in real estate. After all, they don't pay you unless you sell! (No disrespect intended to my real estate comrades.) Although the door of entry is easy, it is circular in style, and many revolve around and back out the exit rather quickly. But that career choice worked out much better than I anticipated. I was rookie of the year for the largest company in Wisconsin in 1993, despite not getting started until July. Within a year I had bought a house, a new car, met my soon-to-be bride and soon thereafter, I was a young man with money and unable to manage it. Worst yet, I still had no real sense of purpose.

At this time, the office I worked at was managed by this really delightfully "weird" lady. Her name was Mary Steinke. She was a bright light, and the way she conducted herself was very unlike nearly anyone I had previously met. She had joy. She seemed to have a higher purpose. Although she took her job seriously, she did it with a smile and always carried herself as though there was something bigger going on than a real estate transaction. I learned she was a Christian, and soon I learned that many others in the office also were Christians. They tried sharing things with me, and although I had some curiosity, I was too busy making money and living the American dream to deeply consider what they were saying, at least at first. My motto was: Work hard and play hard.

I got married in December of 1995. I remember praying to a God that I was not even sure existed to bless my marriage. After getting married, I started reading the Bible. Uh oh! That's a dangerous thing to do; as God has said, when you seek, you shall find. Somebody told me to read the Gospel of John, so I did, and I really started gaining curiosity about what I was reading. Initially, however, when I read John, I was confused. John the author begins by talking about another John in the first chapter of his book, and I didn't know who was who. That is when I bought a six-hour movie titled *Jesus of Nazareth*. I felt like God woke me up—sometimes in the middle of the night!—to tell me to put that movie on. It is really done well from a first-century, historic perspective. It is not a movie that a contemporary person would love if they are looking for a typical Hollywood-style, action-packed movie. However, if you want to get a picture of what Jesus and the world looked like at that time, and you desire to seek God, I recommend it. After watching this film, I would pick up the Bible, and I now had a visual picture in my mind of what I was reading. It made the Scriptures come alive for me, and I could now see who John the Baptist was, as compared with John the Apostle.

There were two things going on inside my mind at this time. One was that I was afraid to die. I used to think about dying and being put into a casket, but my casket had a window in the top of it. I possess the "type A" personality, and at that time loved to water ski, golf, hunt, play basketball, you name it. When I pictured death, I pictured being dead in that casket, but consciously alive and able to see out the window in the top, unable to move. I visualized being put down into the ground in my casket, and there was still light coming through the window. Then, slowly, the light went away, one shovel of dirt at a time, until there was nothing but darkness. My Hell at that time was imagining being alive, six feet deep, in that casket, with no possibility of ever getting out. Needless to say, I was afraid to die. Yet I was not overly troubled by this because, like most young people, whenever I thought about death,

I did not like those thoughts, so I mastered doing whatever I could to not think about it. Stuff it, suppress it—whatever I could do to go back to living my life, my way. But as I suspect you know, I could not escape my own mind. One's thoughts tend to boomerang. The second thought I was wrestling with was even more profound.

I began to ponder why I was taking up air.

I was in my midtwenties and I had bought a car and a house, had a pretty wife, and I had a good income. Is that not the purpose of life? Feeling like I had started to achieve what the world told me was significant left me thinking there had to be more. I have had to struggle with finances much more as I've aged than when I was young. Earlier in life I had a basketball court in my home, lived on a golf course with a membership, and had my own golf cart. It is not news that struggling with finances is not fun. However, what I am about to say is confirmed by the news that you see and read every day. We see it all the time. People who have money many times struggle finding fulfillment. Oh, at first glance they may give the appearance of being fulfilled, but wealthy people who do not have an understanding of life's purpose are just as troubled as anyone else. The problem is that when one has money it can take that person longer to realize they very well may be lost. Money can disguise one's true need—even to oneself.

Why am I taking up air? Have you ever thought of that? I encourage you to do so as you read this book. Why are you taking up air? Is there purpose to life? Reaching subconscious goals that Americans have at a young age made me wonder: Are the purposes in life success, possessions, and living for the American dream? Somehow I knew—or rather I believed—that God should get the credit for impressing on me, and that as I began to seek Him, that there must be more to life. I was not an unhappy person. It is easier to distract yourself when you have the money to do so. But I could not shake the thought that boomeranged in my mind:

Is there purpose to living above and beyond the American dream, and if so, what is it?

It was now the fall of 1996, I had been married for eight months, and my wife and I were thinking about having a family. That thought prompted us to think about going to church. Our reasoning was that when we had a child we would then have a church. Our parents had taken us as kids, and it seemed like the right thing to do. I had decided that the traditional church did not help me to understand God, or have much faith in Him, so I was not compelled to go back there. A client of mine was one of the first people to invite us to church, so we went and checked it out. It was a nondenominational, Bible-based church. I had not been to a church like this before, so I was simply taking it all in. It started with musical worship, and what struck me was the realness I sensed about the worship. I was used to people who barely opened their mouths, and then when they did, they looked like lifeless robots. I was one of them. But many people at this place seemed to sing from a place in their hearts of which I was not yet aware in my own heart. A few had their eyes closed, and a couple had their hands up. Although that was new to me, I was OK with it, and the music was pretty good too. After worship was over, the pastor asked people to open their Bibles. I had just started reading one, but I had no idea I was to bring it to church. I would not know how to find anything anyway! The lady next to me opened her Bible, and I was looking at her Bible out of the corner of my eye so that she would not know I was looking. She had that Bible highlighted with manifold colors and neatly underlined, and I was thinking, *Wow, this lady really reads that thing.* That is all I remembered from that service, but it was enough to leave an impression on me to this day.

We started going most weeks, and I continued reading the Bible. One Thursday night in October of 1996, my wife and I were at our home tucked in the woods of the Kettle Moraine Forest. There was a knock on our door. It was rare to have a visitor in our forested area, especially at 7 p.m. I went to the door, and there were some smiling faces whom I did not recognize. They let us know that they were visiting from the church we had started to attend, and said they wanted to welcome us. Since we did not want to be rude, and we liked the church, we let them in. After chit-chatting for a little while, they very comfortably and gently asked us some questions. It led to a deep and heartfelt discussion about spiritual things. That night, they articulated to my wife and me, in a way that we had never heard that clearly before, what is known as the Gospel. They then asked us if we desired to place our trust in Jesus Christ as our Lord and Savior. Although we were very green in our full understanding of the Bible, we felt spiritually led to make a decision to trust in Jesus Christ as Lord and Savior. We learned that night that we were sinners, and that our sin separated us from God, who wanted a relationship with us. We placed our trust in the understanding that night that God, in His love, sent His Son, Jesus, to be the one who gave His life as an offering, on a cross, for our sins. Through faith in His death and resurrection, our sin was placed on Him, and we received the forgiveness of sins and the promise of eternal life.

Perhaps you have heard that before, and maybe it makes some sense, but you still have questions. Questions like: Can you believe that? Can you trust that this is true? I believe this book will help answer questions and illustrate powerful evidence that confirms it is true. In the end I will give you the same opportunity that they gave us. That night, God began to change our lives. I remember sensing that I was beginning to become a new person. I remember God speaking to my mind and heart as I read His Word and jogged through the forest. I was eager and excited to know Him more. The fear of death that suffocated my thinking, that I attempted to suppress, was now defeated. I had reason to believe. I was excited that when this temporary tent of a body and short life on earth is done, what lies ahead is a healthy body and eternity in Heaven. This gave me much more peace and joy than money did. Money will be left behind. Prior to this, I was a recreational marijuana smoker. One month later I was going on my annual deer hunt with some friends. On the Friday prior to opening day of hunting, we would typically set up our tree stands and maybe smoke a bowl in the process. I remember wondering if I should do it or not, and I recall feeling a sense that I shouldn't, but I took a hit anyway. That was the last time I ever smoked pot. His Spirit now began to work in me, helping me to not only discern His ways in a variety of areas, but to have His strength to follow through.

I spent the next eight years, eleven in all, selling real estate and developing subdivisions. Toward the end of that time, my goal was to continue to make a fortune, retire early, and be able to both play a lot of golf and do ministry. But one vice that I did not give up immediately was gambling. I used to enjoy casinos and would find one three to four times a year. After I started making good money, I took that desire to the stock market. In 1998 and 1999 I thought I was pretty smart. I opened an E-trade account and was making easy money with a lot of naiveté; after all, that was an easy market to make money in. My pride was large. I thought: *I am going to make a bundle and then go into ministry!* I had a high-risk tolerance. I started buying on margin (borrowing against my stock account to buy more stock), and not only that, I was trying to hit home runs by buying a large amount of a few specific stocks. One stock I had been making a lot of money in was Zomax. This leads to an interesting question.

When it comes to money, when does one have enough?

For most, and for myself at that time, I believe the answer is... just a little bit more. Although I sincerely wanted to go into ministry, I was going about it the wrong way. I was not honoring God with the way I managed money. The Bible talks specifically against such "get rich quick" (Proverbs 13:11) schemes. In addition, the Bible says that "pride comes before the fall" (Proverbs 16:18). And I was about to fall.

One night, Zomax, which had already split, closed at $18 per share. I owned a bunch, both with my own money and through borrowed money on margin. The next day, as I remember it, it opened at $8. It did not even trade in-between. I had seen this stock go up and down so many times that I thought I would hang in there. It ended up dropping much further. That night, and over the next few months, I lost several hundred thousand dollars. To make matters worse, these losses did not even offset some development income that I had assumed would be taxed as capital gains. A few months later I found out that I owed $100,000 in taxes, money I no longer had. I still remember getting off the phone with the accountant, and at that moment, when I realized the full measure of my folly, I wept...loudly. Within thirty minutes of finding this out, I had to take one of my kids to a music class. I was completely in shock, stunned. My life was about to change. In the class I felt like I was in a coma of some strange kind. We had to sell our home to pay our taxes. This was an incredibly valuable experience, and one that God used to make substantial changes in our lives.

I ended up studying all that God has to say about money. I closed my E-trade account and only invested in the future with the help of professionals, and almost completely in mutual funds, which are considered a much safer alternative, compared with my previous reckless habits. God took gambling away from my life. Now, to be honest, I will still play a two-dollar or five-dollar Nassau game with you on the golf course. I'll play sheephead for dimes or quarters, but I have not been to a casino since 1999. What was once a tragedy has now become one of my biggest blessings. You see, the thing about money is that when it is one's idol, more will always be wanted. The reality was that although I wanted to go into ministry, I am not sure I would have ever pulled the trigger. It takes a lot of money to support oneself. I was still a long way from that goal. I guess God had two ways of getting me into ministry. One was to bless me abundantly and hope I had the wisdom to use it properly. Since he knew otherwise, he did the next best thing. He stripped it all away.

In 2003, the Lord led me into full-time ministry, and now I was much better prepared.

When one starts looking at how God is working in his or her life, through their hardships, one can then begin to see the wisdom of God and praise Him in all circumstances. I approached the company I sold for and told them God was calling me into ministry and that I had a plan to transition my real estate team of seven agents into an office for the company. At first the company declined, but later the leaders changed their minds. I want to share this full story, but will pass for the sake of time. In short, they hired me for the last year as a manager, to grow the office I had developed for my team and to make it into a corporate office. It was profitable in its first year. A year later I was in full-time ministry. That was eleven years ago.

It has been quite an adventure. In 2006 I started a youth campus discipleship ministry, called Campus Way. You can look it up if you want to find out more. We help churches launch community/campus-based youth and children's ministries to students in their local school districts. Praise God, more than 160 individual decisions have been made by students to trust in Christ, through that ministry, just like I once did. In 2009, with the prompting of God, we planted a church, now called Brandybrook Christian Church. On top of starting two ministries and being the father of three kids, I also made time to complete a Masters-level Christian Studies certification through Trinity Divinity in Deerfield, Illinois. Going from what we had, financially, to now eleven years of ministry income has been tremendously more difficult than what I would have anticipated. Despite that, I cannot shake the awesome purpose that God gives to the lives of those who follow Him. Many lives have been impacted by the ministries we lead, and I remind myself regularly that people who now have Jesus and His promised treasure of eternal life are far more valuable than the earthly treasure that, if I'm honest, I still miss.

Here is the reason I believe God led me to write this book.

There are many people in the world (and friends in my life) that I have never gained an audience long enough to present the evidence that would help them discover the love of God. Not only is it difficult to gain an audience of busy people in my own community, it would be impossible for me to gain an audience long enough with each person around the world to share with them this crucial evidence. This book is the result of God prompting me to do my part to get His evidence shared and His purpose known.

Some old secular friends and I get together, nearly annually, for a time of friendship and golf. We call this event the Colorado/ Wisconsin Cup. More than a year ago I asked some of my friends this question: "If I wrote you a book about how I learned to trust in God and how he called me into ministry, would you read it?" They answered yes, and since that day I have been determined to get this into their hands, as well as into the hands of many others I care about. God knows, and they know, I have tried to share with them a testimony about God both on the golf course and in the course of life. I have followed through, and I humbly long that you will follow through on reading this book until its emphatic close.

For all of you, one day I hope to embrace my friends, and the readers of this book, not merely in an earthly embrace, but in the everlasting hug of friendship for those who have inherited the same eternal destiny because of the faith they have placed in God.

The purpose of this book is to convince people there is a source of truth about a God who sent a Savior to a rescue a people who desperately need to be rescued, and that once saved we have great purpose in becoming rescuers ourselves. Although God is the ultimate Hero, we get to be His agent and also a hero in someone else's life. In becoming a rescuer lies an awesome purpose...and a reason to wake up and take up air.

Questions for Discussion

1) How does your story of faith resemble (or not resemble) the author's? What is an aspect or two that might be similar? What is something that is very different?

2) The author shared the story about how God used the loss of money for good. It helped prompt Jay to go into ministry, probably much sooner than he would have otherwise. Do you have any examples of how God used something that may have appeared bad, for a season, as a good thing that helped shape your life?

3) The author shared that a question he wrestled with was "why are you taking up air"? By the end of the book it is hoped you will be further along the journey of exploring how God wants to use you. In fact, it is hoped that your small group will assist one another in this discovery. Does anyone have a thought on what they believe their Kingdom purpose might be?

Chapter Four

Opening Evidence

In this book we will explore the theme of an offering, which is weaved throughout the story of the Bible. This theme will provide us with both rich understanding and display for us evidence that God has had a plan from the beginning. An additional way an offering is described biblically is through the word "presenting"—the presenting of a sacrifice. Through this biblical theme of presenting an offering, we will gain a picture that will help us understand the Gospel of Jesus Christ and God's desired response from us to that message. My hope is that the image of an offering will forever be stamped in our hearts and minds to strengthen our resolve to follow Him forever.

Before I proceed to display the imagery of an offering and the critical importance of it, I first want to provide evidence as to why we can trust in the message. This book is based on the message of the Bible; therefore, it is important that we gain an understanding of why the Bible can be trusted. I realize (and even hope) that there are many reading who, at this point, question their trust of the Bible. If indeed there are readers of this book that question the Bible's trustworthiness, it is being read by the right audience. One of the reasons many distrust the Bible is because they may have not yet obtained the local knowledge of the ocean, so to speak (to return to our chapter 1 metaphor), which, if they knew, would help them evade the rip current of public opinion that is pulling people away from trusting God and His Word. I think we would all agree that before making judgment on a very important matter, it would first be wise to examine the evidence. There seems to be a common belief that intelligent people reject faith. The reality is, when one has *more knowledge* regarding the Bible's reliability, one will have increased faith.

Many people who were raised going to church, and who can recount the story of Noah, or David and Goliath, assume that because they know some stories, and went to church as a child, that they then know the Bible. Sadly, some then go on to assume that those small nuggets of knowledge qualify them to make their own determination on the Bible's trustworthiness. I have had many people tell me how they know the Bible and "have practically read the whole thing," or even that their dad was a pastor or mom went to church and taught Sunday school, as though they were then automatically given the deposit of a lifetime of biblical knowledge. Sometimes I humbly ask them the following question to gauge their knowledge: "Do you know what John 3:16 says?" Now, John 3:16 is perhaps the most famous and well-known Bible verse in the world, and rightfully so, as it is a great one. Some of these same people who "know the Bible" have no idea what the verse says, or even where to find it. What's the point of what I am saying? My hope is to help people evaluate their presuppositions regarding their current "true knowledge" and perhaps open their minds to pursue more. To be humble and simply acknowledge, "You know what, I really have not studied the Bible or taken much time to examine the evidence. If the Bible is true, I would like to know what it says." That is a refreshing place to be, and the kind of mind-set in which God can begin to influence one's life. After all, the Bible indicates that Heaven and Hell are at stake. If that is true, the value of proper knowledge is then greater than any earthly possession because we're talking about eternity. More knowledge leads to trust and faith, and faith is what ultimately opens the door to Heaven. Therefore, proper knowledge is needed. The Bible speaks to this directly, and even gives us a warning in order to compel us to gain more.

"My people are destroyed for lack of knowledge;..."

(HOSEA 4:6, ESV)

I believe God is pleased with a person's effort to read this book and, ultimately, *His* book. In doing so they are being wise by examining the evidence. There is a map, and the map indeed leads to a treasure. The treasure is life with God now and eternal life forever, but in order to receive the treasure one needs to follow the map. If I told someone there was a treasure and gave them a map to find it, they would need to trust and follow the map in order to find those valuable goods. So my job at the onset, and throughout this book, is to show people the accuracy of the map so they can inherit the treasure that lasts forever. I will now begin with the opening statement in our trial to help the "jurors" examine whether the Bible is true.

When Jesus was on earth, He recruited twelve men to follow Him. All the authors of the New Testament were either one of these eyewitnesses to His life or someone directly influenced by them. It's interesting to note that nearly every one of these men has a historical, written record of being martyred for their faith in Jesus. These men claimed to live with, eat with, do ministry with, and have special revelation from Jesus, and many saw Him die and then rise again after His death. A person has two options. They can either believe these men are telling the truth about Jesus, or convince themselves that these authors were making it all up. I would affirm, however, that being martyred, by itself, is not sufficient enough evidence, as people have been martyred for other faiths. But here is where it gets interesting. As mentioned, many of these men were eyewitnesses to Jesus' life, death, and resurrection. So allow me to ask a straightforward question. If these men were "making up" this story that they indeed saw Jesus after His death, would they *know* they were making it up? Of course they would. If they were lying, they would know they were lying. So here is an interesting question: If they were lying, and they knew they were lying, *why would they die for a lie?* Why would they not simply tell the truth and deny the resurrected Christ and live, rather than die for a lie? Yet there is not one historical document claiming that these men ever denied the Christ, even when they were being martyred for their faith. Do you see? These men were eyewitnesses of Jesus' resurrection, and they could not deny what they saw with their own eyes. They believed so much that they were willing to die for Jesus so we could learn of His life, death, resurrection and, ultimately, have His Word, the Bible.

Most of us "slightly older folks" are able to remember the famous O.J. Simpson case from 1995. For those of you who are younger than I, Simpson was a famous retired football player who was charged with the murders of his ex-wife, Nichole Brown Simpson, and Ron Goldman. I remember watching on live television as Simpson's white Bronco was galloping down the highway as helicopters followed above. For you young folks, this was one of the first times in our generation that we had live coverage of something like this. After he was apprehended, it ended up being one of the most famous trials of all time. Nearly everyone born before, say, about 1980 will remember this famous line from a Simpson defense attorney during the trial: "If the glove doesn't fit, you must acquit!" The attorney claimed that the gloves—which police and prosecutors claimed were used by O.J. while committing the murders—were supposedly too small to fit on his large hands. Frankly speaking, I have squeezed my hands into one of my kid's small gloves many times when I was too lazy to keep looking for my own! Somehow, incredibly, Simpson was found not guilty by jury in this criminal trial. And this leads to a good question. Above all else, why did Simpson get off? One intelligent response I sometimes hear is that the public, and the jurors, were swayed by his fame. Another response many times heard is that he had money and, as a result, could hire excellent lawyers. Some of that, I am sure, influenced the situation, but there is a far more compelling reason that Simpson was acquitted. No, I don't believe it was his fame, or his money, or simply because he had better lawyers, or even the fact that the gloves "didn't fit." So then, what was it?

No one saw him do it.

Go down this path with me for a moment. What if *one person* saw him do it? What would O.J.'s lawyers have done? They would have attempted everything possible to discredit that single witness. Maybe he still would have got off, if there had only been one witness who saw him kill his ex-wife, but probably, that would have been enough to get a guilty verdict. Let's carry this a little further. What if two people saw him do it? Surely the lawyers would try to discredit both of them, but now it is getting significantly more difficult for them to win the defense. What if three witnesses saw him do it? What about ten? He would have been toast! What if five hundred people saw O.J. Simpson murder his wife and the other man? He would not have stood a chance. He would have been found guilty as charged. All of us, including that jury, would have been overwhelmingly convinced at the evidence of five hundred witnesses. There may not have even been a trial! My brothers and sisters on this earth, in this thing called life, Jesus came back to life for a period of forty days and showed himself, including the holes in His hands and the spear mark in His side. He not only showed Himself to his disciples, who never denied it—even to the point of death—but the Bible teaches us that He showed himself alive to more than five hundred people after his death.

The Bible verse I will share below was written by Paul, who became one of the Lord's apostles, and who also was martyred for his faith. Paul was a pretty remarkable guy. He was a Jewish leader who hated the spread of Christianity. He was so dedicated to his cause that he was taking Christians to prison and even approving of their death. This all happened not long after Jesus ascended into Heaven. One day, Jesus, seeing from Heaven this very zealous man, seemed to come to the conclusion that instead of this man opposing him, He needed this kind of zeal on the right team. One day, Paul, still on his mission to take down the spread of Christianity, was approached by a huge, bright light from Jesus, who spoke to him and even caused Paul to lose his sight! Days later, Jesus had Paul's sight restored and radically began to transform this man by the power of God. Paul, through this conversion, was given a totally new purpose in life, one to now live for: the mission of God. Paul ended up becoming one of the greatest missionaries of all time.

Jesus is still radically changing lives today. He has done it for me and He can do it for you. You can read this story about Paul for yourself, in Acts 9, in the Bible. But be careful! The Bible says that when a person seeks, they will find (Jeremiah 29:13). Paul was alive at the time of Jesus' death, and his ministry took place over the next thirty-five years. Here is what Paul wrote about the resurrection of Jesus.

The Resurrection of Christ

Now I would remind you, brothers, of the gospel
I preached to you, which you received, in which you stand,
and by which you are being saved, if you hold fast to the
word I preached to you—unless you believed in vain.

For I delivered to you as of first importance what I also received: that Christ died for our sins in accordance with the Scriptures, that he was buried, that he was raised on the third day in accordance with the Scriptures, and that he appeared to Cephas, then to the twelve. Then he appeared to more than five hundred brothers at one time, most of whom are still alive, though some have fallen asleep. Then he appeared to James, then to all the apostles. Last of all, as to one untimely born, he appeared also to me. For I am the least of the apostles, unworthy to be called an apostle, because I persecuted the church of God.

(1 CORINTHIANS 15:1-9, ESV)

It seems to me that this man, who died for his faith, is telling the truth. Before we move on, I want to share with you one more of Jesus' resurrection appearances. On one of these appearances after his death, Jesus visited with ten of His twelve apostles. One of the twelve, Judas Iscariot, who betrayed Jesus, soon after the betrayal took his own life, in what appears to be regret over his decision. On this, the very first Easter Sunday, after the cross of Good Friday, Jesus showed up in a home where ten of the remaining apostles were present. They were overjoyed to see Him alive again. But one of the apostles, Thomas, was not there. Here is what happened next.

Jesus and Thomas

Now Thomas, one of the Twelve, called the Twin, was not with them when Jesus came. So the other disciples told him, "We have seen the Lord." But he said to them, "Unless I see in his hands the mark of the nails, and place my finger into the mark of the nails, and place my hand into his side, I will never believe."

(JOHN 20:24, 25, ESV)

43

I am not going to judge Thomas. I can understand. Have you ever seen someone come back from the dead? It is understandable that Thomas would have a hard time believing.

But check out what happened next.

Eight days later, his disciples were inside again, and Thomas was with them. Although the doors were locked, Jesus came and stood among them and said, "Peace be with you."
Then he said to Thomas,
"Put your finger here, and see my hands; and put out your hand, and place it in my side. Do not disbelieve, but believe."
Thomas answered him, "My Lord and my God!"
Jesus said to him,
"Have you believed because you have seen me?
Blessed are those who have not seen and yet have believed."
(JOHN 20:26-29, ESV)

Amazing! Do you realize Jesus, who spoke these words, is referring to you and me when He says, "Blessed are those who have not seen and yet have believed." He later showed himself to His apostles on several more occasions and then, ultimately, to five hundred more. This leaves us with a powerful question.

If five hundred people saw O.J. Simpson kill his wife, would you have had to see it, personally, to believe?

Now let's take it a step further. Let's just say twelve people saw O.J. kill his wife, but then those witnesses were put to the test, because it was believed they were lying. Next comes an ultimatum to those witnesses: "We don't believe you. If you will deny what you say you saw, we may then allow you to live. If you continue to purport this lie, we are going to take your life. Now answer us clearly: did you see Mr. Simpson kill his ex-wife?" Now if they were indeed lying about seeing O.J. kill his ex-wife, I don't think they would take more than a second to simply tell the truth and escape death. Jesus' apostles were willing to die for proclaiming what they believed in their hearts and saw with their own eyes. They did not, and could not, deny the resurrection of Christ.

I am thankful that Jesus displayed patience and compassion to come back and show himself to Thomas, who doubted. Thomas was our representative, but now Jesus is desiring that like Thomas, we would believe. It requires faith. But not blind faith. There is ample evidence, and we have just begun. Significantly more evidence will be revealed throughout this book. The apostle John, one of the apostles in that room when Jesus came back to show Thomas, also died in an interesting way. He was essentially imprisoned on an island called Patmos, where he was able to write, but where he eventually would die. He wrote an account of the life, death, and resurrection of Jesus. Near the end of his book he shares his purpose in writing. I humbly join him in the same purpose.

Now Jesus did many other signs in the presence of the disciples,

which are not written in this book;

but these are written so that you may believe that

Jesus is the Christ, the Son of God,

and that by believing you may have life in his name.

(JOHN 20:30, 31, ESV)

Questions for Discussion

1) When it comes to faith, how important is knowledge of the Bible, and why?

2) If you wrote a book to your child, how would you feel when you saw them reading it? What do you think God is thinking when we begin to seek Him through reading the Bible, or even reading through a Christian book like this one?

3) How does the testimony of the disciples and their martyrdom impact your faith?

4) What are some other evidences of Jesus that you aware of that help build your faith?

5) The chapter closes with John 20:30, 31. What encouragement do you find in those verses?

Chapter Five

Why We Need a Rescuer

What is the purpose of God for mankind, and why do we need to be rescued?

In some ways this chapter is not only the most difficult, but also the most important. Imagine for a moment approaching a perfectly healthy person and randomly saying to them, "You are cancer-free." They would probably look at you puzzled, and perhaps respond by saying, "Umm, is there something I should know?" Now, imagine a patient in a hospital room, who had just undergone extensive cancer treatments. The patient's doctor, upon entering the room, announces with a smile: "You are cancer-free!!" The patient would not only have a huge sigh of relief, but likely tears of thankfulness and joy. This illustrates something important. Good news is that much better when one knows just how bad the bad news can be. In the opening of this book we began with a story about some people who were caught in an ocean rip current and needed to be rescued. Unfortunately, they did not know they needed to be rescued—until it was too late. It can be hard to rescue a person who does not think he needs rescuing. I can't wait to tell more of the story of our God and the good news that He is a rescuer, but first, all people (including myself!) need to have a clear understanding of why we need to be rescued.

In the first book of the Bible, called Genesis, God creates man and woman. There are some very important foundational lessons to be learned from this part of God's story. The first has to do with our purpose. The second has to do with our problem.

We are about to discover what I call the Grand Purpose of God. What is God after? What is He trying to accomplish? What is the purpose of mankind? These are really important questions, and although they are not the central focus of this book, it is important to understand the answers to these questions so that we can understand God better. One knows a person much better when they know that person's motive.

When God created Adam and Eve, He gave them a mission. It is the first commission of God to mankind.

> Then God said, "Let us make man in our <u>image</u>,
> after our <u>likeness</u>. And let them have dominion
> over the fish of the sea and over the
> birds of the heavens and over
> the livestock and over all the earth
> and over every creeping thing that creeps on the earth."
> So God created man in his own <u>image</u>,
> in the <u>image</u> of God he created him;
> male and female he created them.
> And God blessed them. And God said to them,
> "<u>Be fruitful and multiply</u>..."
> (GENESIS 1:26-28, ESV)

In this passage, I have provided emphasis (underlined) for the points that I believe are critical to illustrate. God made man and woman in His image and likeness, and then gave them His mission to be fruitful by multiplying that image and likeness in people throughout the earth. Isn't it true that as people we multiply much of who we are? My wife and I will sometimes tease each other about some of the tendencies we have that are so similar to those of our parents. In addition, we recognize some of our children's behaviors that resemble our own. Fortunately or unfortunately, we multiply who we are. With God's help, our kids can overcome some of the deficiencies we pass along to them, and with His help there are some good things we pass on to our children as well. For example, my middle daughter has a drive to succeed athletically and a determination to work at things, but she also likes to irritate her mom (like her father) by leaving a path of destruction wherever she goes. Yes, for better or worse, we multiply who we are. As we will see in a moment, this was also true in the lives of Adam and Eve. But first we need to see God's purpose more clearly.

God gave Adam and Eve a beautiful garden in which to begin their lives. They were naked and felt no shame. Knowing man's nature and the beauty of woman, I am thinking it did not take long for them to figure out how to come together. However, it is it not just the multiplication of offspring that God desires. Much later in the New Testament, when Jesus met with His apostles on one of his last postresurrection visits, He gave them what is known as the Great Commission.

"Go therefore and make disciples of all nations, ..."
(MATTHEW 28:19, ESV)

This is highly regarded and portrayed as the New Testament's primary mission that God gave to His followers. God's mission statements in both New and Old Testaments can be woven together beautifully in what I call the Grand Purpose of God.

The Grand Purpose of God is that we become a greater reflection of His image and likeness and be fruitful by multiplying His image and likeness in people throughout the nations.

God is so very pleased when we seek Him, seek to love like Him, seek to live life with His priorities, and obey His desires. In God's economy, people are of the utmost value. His desire is that people throughout the world know Him and make Him known. By knowing Him and His ways, they can live a blessed life with His guidance. As we seek to reflect who He is and what He is like to others, we can then help others have a life that is also blessed by knowing Him and making Him known. We do this both through our offspring and through the relationships we develop with others. As we raise our children to follow God, and intentionally set an example of following God, and His ways, in front of our friends and family, we are living to honor God's purpose. We should purposely try to reflect more of what God is like to others and encourage them to do likewise. This is what God is after. A world of people in love with Him and perpetuating His goodness. Unfortunately, man has struggled to succeed in this mission. We are about to find out why.

When Adam first saw Eve, the Bible records him saying *"this at last"* is "bone of my bones and flesh of my flesh!" (Genesis 2:23, ESV). I picture Adam saying, "Wow! Praise the Lord," as he looked at Eve. The very next words shared by God were that man shall leave his father and mother and cleave to his wife and the two become one flesh. The Bible records that this man and his wife were both naked and felt no shame. God wanted multiplication, and I am thinking it may not have taken Adam and Eve long, with no clothes on, to figure that out!

There is something else very important to note. At this time in history God was present with Adam and Eve in the garden and spoke to them in that place several times. God's desire was not to be distant, but rather to have a close relationship with man. If that were not His desire, He would not have created a garden for the three of them to enjoy together.

Sadly, it did not take man long to ruin a good thing; something was about to get in the way. God gave man very few rules, but He did give the couple one important one. He told them He had planted a tree in middle of the garden: the tree of the knowledge of good and evil. He instructed them clearly that they should not eat from that tree.

So now we have Adam and Eve, in an awesome garden, in relationship with God, and nothing yet creating a problem in that relationship. Just one rule . . . and much like us, we have a hard time passing up the cookie jar even though we know we should. In the biblical story, Eve, and then Adam, were tempted by Satan to eat from this tree. In so many words, he said: "It will not be that bad. Relax, it's not that big of a deal. Just give it a try. A little can't hurt." Let's look closely at Satan's strategy and specifically at what he said; there is something powerful to learn from it. Satan said, "Did God actually say you were not to eat of that tree?" (Genesis 3:1, ESV). He goes on to convince Eve, and then Adam, that it will be OK. Now we need to really think about this. God said something. God spoke Words. God shared these Words with man and He wanted man to trust in His Words. What was Satan's tactic? Do you see? Satan got man to question whether he could trust in God's Word. That is still his tactic today, and many have fallen for it. I hope this book infuses all who read it with renewed confidence that God desires us to believe in His Word.

Like Adam and Eve, all of us likely have fallen into the trap of justifying sin. Unfortunately, that sin, which seems innocent at first, eventually catches up with us. When we sin against each other, it divides relationships. If you steal from me, I will not be pleased with you. If a person cheats on their spouse, it will, at the very least, hinder for a time, and may even break the relationship. So Adam and Eve ate of the tree and broke God's one rule. In short, Adam and Eve sinned against God. Adam and Eve, until this moment, were with God in the garden and were naked and felt no shame. Immediately after this sin they put on clothes and hid themselves from God. Sin hates light and loves darkness. Think about it: much sin is done at night and in private. When man sins, he tries to hide from God. Have you ever played hide-and-seek with a child by placing your hands over their eyes? A young child begins to learn that even though a hand is over their eyes and they cannot see, they can still be seen. At first they don't get this. As adults, sometimes we are like that child. We forget something. You cannot beat God in a game of hide-and-seek. He knows our hiding place. When we sin, we hide by not attending church or by not reading our Bible or by avoiding people who love God. Sin separates us from the God who desires a relationship with us.

Now that Adam and Eve sinned, there were many consequences. Man, who was innocent, and had it made, now knew both good and evil and had become marked with that evil, called sin. It had now become part of man's nature. The consequence was that Adam and Eve were now banned from the garden and the close presence of God, because God and sin do not go together.

This separated God from the relationship he desired with Adam and Eve, and when man is not in close relationship with God, man's sinfulness tends to get worse. This chapter began with the premise that we multiply who we are. Adam and Eve were now multiplying, and they had two boys, Cain and Abel. As we share the story of Cain and Abel, we will also begin to be introduced to the theme of an "offering," which is both an important part of this book and is woven throughout the historical record of the Scriptures. As the boys Cain and Abel grew up, they must have been taught to bring an offering to God. We know this because, as they grow older, the Bible records them bringing an offering to God. Abel offered the firstborn of his flock and Cain offered some fruit. The Bible indicates that God looked very favorably upon Abel's offering of the firstborn of his flock, yet not so favorably on Cain's offering of fruit. This is interesting and will make more sense as this book develops. For now, let's just note that God, very early in the account of His story with man, looks favorably on the sacrifice of a firstborn. Unfortunately, Cain became angry that his offering did not receive the favor that Abel's did. The Lord tried to comfort Cain by saying:

"Why are you so angry and why has your face fallen?

If you do well, will you not be accepted?

And if you do not do well,

sin is crouching at the door.

Its desire is for you, but you must rule over it."

(GENESIS 4:6a, 7, ESV)

Unfortunately, Cain did not heed the warning. So Cain, with the sinful tendencies passed on to him from his parents, handled this very poorly. A simple argument was not enough for Cain; he did something far more grievous. Cain...*killed Abel.* Ugh...sin is on the loose.

Adam and Eve, who knew no evil and were made in the image and likeness of God and had been given the command to be fruitful and multiply, did the latter (multiplied) after staining the former (the image and likeness). Oh yes, they multiplied as they were told, but instead of multiplying the image and likeness of God, they multiplied sin. Ever since this time, all mankind, including you and I, have struggled with sin. The apostle Paul teaches us this very point.

Therefore, just as sin came into the world through one man,
and death through sin, and so death
spread to all men because all sinned...
(ROMANS 5:12, ESV)

...one trespass led to condemnation for all men, ...
(ROMANS 5:18, ESV)

These verses teach us that sin came into the world through one man, and through this one man, Adam, condemnation came for all men. From that day forward all people, all the way up to our current day, struggle with sin. In the first book of the Bible, Genesis, we see that when man became sinful we were separated from the garden. In the last book of the Bible, Revelation (in chapters 21 and 22), we see that there will be a new Heaven and a new earth with a new tree of life. Just like the garden was to be without sin, we learn that Heaven too is a place without sin.

We are now ready to link the introduction of this book to the Bible's teaching. We are in danger of not making it to Heaven because Heaven and sin do not mix and we *all* have inherited Adam's sin since we've all participated in sin and made it our own. The Bible confirms this when it tells us that "all have sinned and fallen short of the Glory of God" (Romans 3:23, ESV). All means *all*. That includes the author of this book, all who read it, and all who don't. We will now see how pervasive this sin problem became. You may remember the story of Noah, which happens a bit down the road in history from Adam and Eve. Many know that God flooded the earth and Noah built an ark, or huge boat, but many do not know the reason why.

The LORD saw that the wickedness of man
was great in the earth, and that every intention
of the thoughts of his heart was only evil continually.

> **And the LORD regretted that he had made man**
> **on the earth, and it grieved him to his heart.**
> **So the LORD said, "I will blot out man whom I have created from**
> **the face of the land, man and animals and creeping things and**
> **birds of the heavens, for I am sorry that I have made them."**
> **But Noah found favor in the eyes of the LORD.**
> (GENESIS 6:5-8, ESV)

When man failed to multiply God's image because of sin, God elected to start over through Noah. That mission to multiply His image in man was not just words. He meant it. So after a massive flood and a really long time on the ark, eventually the waters receded from the earth. When Noah got off the ark, God spoke to him and gave Noah a mission. It is interesting to note that Noah had just been miraculously rescued by God. After more than a year of tested patience on that ark, Noah, now on dry ground, had to be incredibly thankful to have survived the flood and to be selected by God to be the lone surviving family. Finally, at last, he was on dry ground. God had rescued him. When Noah got off the ark, it is interesting to note the very first thing he did.

> **Then Noah built an altar to the LORD and took some of every**
> **clean animal and some of every clean bird**
> **and offered burnt offerings on the altar.**
> **And when the LORD smelled the pleasing aroma,**
> **the LORD said in his heart,**
> **"I will never again curse the ground**
> **because of man, for the intention of his heart**
> **is evil from his youth. Neither will I ever strike down**
> **every living creature as I have done."**
> (GENESIS 8:20, 21, ESV)

Hmm. Do you remember Abel? God was pleased with his offering, and here again we see that the Lord was pleased with Noah and his offering. The theme of an offering is beginning to be introduced, but at this point, *introduced* is the best way to put it. Despite man's sinfulness even from youth, God is going to start over with Noah, and He promises He will not flood the earth again despite the problem all of us have with sin. So now what is Noah to do? What is God's mission for Noah—and for us?

> **And God blessed Noah and his sons and said to them,**
> **"be fruitful and multiply and fill the earth."...for God made**
> **man in his own image. "And you be fruitful and multiply,**
> **increase greatly on the earth and multiply in it."**
> (GENESIS 9:1, 6b, 7, ESV)

Sound familiar? God has been about that—multiplication—from the time of His creation. He was still after that, now through Noah's family, and He is still desiring that today. Sadly, Noah, although a good man, was like us—far from perfect. Noah, who came from Adam, like us, inherited Adam's sin problem and fell back into sin. Noah did not fare much better than Adam. Sin was still being spread like the flu.

I wonder what God is going to do? What is the solution to this problem?

We are about to work our way out of this darkness and move toward the light. However, I first want to illustrate three important things we have learned.

- First, God has a consistent mission for mankind, to multiply His image and likeness in people throughout the nations.

- Second, through Abel and Noah we are able to see that God is hinting to us that he is pleased with sacrifice. When we give him an offering in appreciation of Him, He is pleased. This dim light will burn brighter as we carry on.

- Third and most profound, Adam, Eve, Cain, Noah, you, and I—we all share the same sin problem. We have all, since this time, inherited and participated in sin. Heaven is a perfect place, and just as Adam and Eve were removed from the garden and from the presence of God, we too are separated from God's future Heaven due to our sin. This is the reason we need to be rescued. Mankind is caught in a rip current of sin that is pulling him away from God. We are never good enough on our own to make it to Heaven because this sin is with us. We are not strong enough to swim against the current. We must embrace the bad news that our sin separates us from God so that we are overjoyed when we hear the good news that there is a way to be saved from our sin through God's rescuer.

Noah was no more successful than Adam in succeeding in multiplying the image of God. But God is not surprised. God is not caught off guard. How is God going to solve this problem? How is God going to restore us to a close relationship with Him despite our sinful tendencies? How is God not only going to rescue us, but also rescue His mission? No, God did not make Heaven just for himself. As I write, a Super Bowl will be played (and completed) later today. The stadium will be full of wild, cheering fans. But that throng will in no way rival the cheers of Heaven from the full stadium of God, filled with those who shout for joy that they have been loved and rescued by God for eternity!

The story of the Bible, the story of God, the story of this book is how God works throughout history in a grand way, with detailed evidence, to display to you and me that this story does not end in darkness, but in light. He has a plan. He has a solution. Our God is a rescuer. Despite our sin He has made a way to rescue us to live for His grand purpose, and to live forever.

Discussion Questions

**This is an important chapter;
be prepared to spend a couple of weeks
in discussion, if needed.**

1) In this chapter we learn that God gives mankind a purpose through the instructions to Adam and Eve. How does the author, and how do you, describe God's purpose for mankind?

2) How should knowing God's purpose shape a person's life?

3) When Adam and Eve were in the garden, where was the presence of God? What does that say about God's desire for a relationship with man and woman?

4) Why did Adam and Eve have to depart from the garden and the direct presence of God?

5) What was Satan's tactic to lead Adam and Eve into sin? What can we learn from this?

6) What did Adam and Eve do immediately after they sinned? How does that compare to people today when they fall into sin? What should we do instead when we fall into sin?

7) Adam and Eve succeeded in multiplying, but what multiplied with them? How does this motivate you in regard to your influence on your family and those around you?

8) Why does every person on earth need to be rescued? (Read Romans 5:12, 18, and Romans 6:23.) How should this motivate us in our relationships?

Chapter Six

The Story of God's People from Noah to Egypt:

The Need for a Passover

There was a man who bought a couch and a painting for his living room from a secondhand shop.[1] Since he had a hole in his living room wall, he hung this painting over the hole to cover it up. Time went by without the man giving much consideration to the picture or the hole. One day, the man was playing a board game. The game is played by picking a card from the deck. Unlike a traditional deck of cards, these cards have pictures of various items of unknown value. The aim of the game is to bid on, and then acquire, the items that are of greatest value. As the man and his friends were playing, a card was picked from the deck that looked rather familiar. It was of a particular painting. The man looked curiously at the card, pondering why it looked so familiar. He thought to himself, *I know I have seen that painting before.* Sure enough, as he peered up at his wall, he recognized that the painting on the wall looked just like the picture on the card. His curiosity consumed him. With a measure of excitement, he shortly thereafter took the painting to an appraiser and discovered that this painting was worth more than a million dollars! Incredible! Oh, how we all wish that would be us!

Reading the Old Testament can be like this. At first glance, the Old Testament can be similar to looking at an unknown item that may seem unassuming, until a later discovery points out that that very item is an ancient, historic artifact of great—even eternal—value. Many people do not know the Old Testament well and, as a result, when a New Testament passage reveals to us some beautiful evidence of our ancient artifact, we, and they, miss it. It's just like that picture on that wall. If the man would have known what he had, he would have benefited from its value long before. It is not that the value was not there, it was that he *did not know the evidence* that leads to understanding, which in turn reveals the value. Sometimes the New Testament authors, who were predominantly Jewish (prior to their conversion to Christianity), did not go out of their way to explain some of their Jewish, Old Testament understanding. They believed, with good reason, that their first-century audience would be able to understand. Today, it is critical that we learn the Old Testament history and view it with a Hebrew/Jewish lens so that when reading we receive the full, eternal value of the artifact. After all, it would be a shame to sell a Babe Ruth rookie baseball card for a dollar because we did not know who he was. In the next several chapters, I am going to display some awesome artifacts that will, at first, seem unassuming. In the later chapters of this book, these artifacts will be revealed for their full importance and eternal value. In the end, it will be shown that there are awesome historical evidences that lend proof that the Bible and the story of this book can be trusted. Rather than stop and explain every artifact now, I will simply be bringing to mind what will later be revealed and then help our faith to thunder in strength.

We will now continue a condensed presentation of Genesis, the first, and one of the most important, books of the Bible. We are on a journey to a massive historical event known as the Passover. After Noah, we meet an old man named Abraham and his elderly wife, Sarah, who have been unable to have their own children. God tells Abraham that through him He is going to multiply God's family to be like the multitude of the stars in the sky. Sounds pretty cool, right? Abraham is supposed to multiply the family of God according to the mission of God that we discussed earlier; however, Abraham has a huge problem. Not only were Sarah and Abraham old, but she was also barren throughout her many years. When God told Abraham that it would be through his wife, Sarah, that he would have a son and multiply this family, Abraham's response was not very honorable. He actually laughed out loud! So there you have it: the very first "lol." To Abraham, this promise seemed too big, even for God. To make matters worse, God gave Abraham this promise in the past, but now it is many years later and this promise still has not come true. To Abraham, it may have appeared the possibility of having a child has passed. Despite the odds being against him Abraham continued to believe in this promise and miraculously God keeps his promise, and Sarah conceives and gives birth to a son. They name him Isaac, which means, fittingly, "laughter."

Some time passed and Isaac now is perhaps a young adolescent. What happens next is truly hard to imagine. One has to place himself in this setting to understand the enormity of what God is about to ask Abraham to do. God, incredibly, asks Abraham to offer this special son, Isaac, as a sacrifice to him. To clarify, in that time, sacrifices made to God were typically a lamb or some other animal. The animal would be slaughtered, and sometimes placed on an altar of stone or wood and then burned. God has now asked Abraham to sacrifice his long-awaited son! It makes no sense whatsoever unless, of course, God has something bigger in mind.

Abraham trusts God so much that he takes Isaac on a hike into the wilderness to "offer a sacrifice" to God.

Do you remember our theme of an offering?

While on this hike, at one point, Isaac, unaware that *he* is to be the sacrifice, asks his father a simple question: "Where are we going to get the sacrifice?" Abraham replies in what later becomes a very fitting response.

Abraham said, "God will provide for himself the lamb

for a burnt offering, my son."

(GENESIS 22:8a, ESV)

For the record, Abraham, like Adam and Noah before him, also had a problem with sin. He had already been caught lying on more than one occasion, according to biblical accounts. It appears he is lying to Isaac to get him to travel with him to the mountaintop and the place of sacrifice. The other option is that maybe God gave him a spiritual revelation that God would indeed somehow provide a solution to this problem. After all, God did say that through Abraham's son, God's family would be multiplied. What was going on in Abraham's mind we are not told. Interestingly, he then has Isaac carry the wood up to the place where Isaac will *himself* become this burnt offering. Upon reaching the mountaintop where the sacrifice is to take place, Abraham, trusting in the Lord, places Isaac on the altar. Mustering something inside himself to obey God, and experiencing something that no father (except God) could understand, he raises the knife to sacrifice his boy, Isaac!

After all, that is typically how a lamb would be slain, by a knife to the throat. Imagine now, Abraham raising the knife and preparing to come down to end the boy's life, and here is what happens next...

But the Angel of the Lord called to him from heaven and said,

"Abraham, Abraham!" And he said, "Here I am." He said,

"Do not lay your hand on the boy or do anything to him,

for I know that you fear God, seeing you have not withheld

your son, your only son, from me. And Abraham lifted up his

eyes and looked, and behold, behind him was a ram,

caught in a thicket by his horns.

And Abraham went and took the ram and offered

it up as a burnt offering instead of his son. So Abraham

called the name of that place, "The Lord will provide; ...."

(GENESIS 22:11-14a, ESV)

Awesome story! Do remember Abraham's words from Genesis 22:8?

Abraham said, "God will provide for himself the lamb

for a burnt offering, my son."

(GENESIS 22:8a, ESV)

It is amazing that his words literally, and miraculously, came true. What is even more incredible is how God beautifully fore-shadows what is to come. God does this foreshadowing through-out the Scriptures. I am only going to hint at this now. In this story God provided a substitute, an animal sacrifice, instead of the boy, Isaac. Many years later when we needed to be rescued, God pro-vided a substitute for us. Like Isaac, it was His one and only son. And just like Isaac, God's Son even carried the wood to the place of sacrifice.

The purpose of this story is to begin to display how God works in His Word to forecast and later fulfill what is to come. In addition, the story begins to bring forth God's solution to man's sin problem that will become so very clear. God is beginning to paint a picture in

His Word regarding the significance of a sacrificial offering. So far, only a corner of the painting is complete; therefore the full beauty of the picture is still, at this point, a mystery. In the end it will be a masterpiece, God's work of art, woven through His Word, to show His plans were beginning to be painted from the beginning of time.

The patriarchs of the Bible, the first family of God's people, are known as the family of Abraham, Isaac, and Jacob. So Abraham has Isaac and Isaac grows up and has a son whom he names Jacob. Jacob (who is also known as Israel), just like Adam, Noah, Abraham, and us, is very imperfect. One of the beautiful things about God is how He patiently uses imperfect people throughout history to see His mission fulfilled. That should be comforting to us. Even though we too struggle with sin, God still desires to use us for His mission.

Jacob goes on to do something every father should know doesn't promote family harmony. He shows great favoritism to one of his many sons, the son named Joseph. He even gives Joseph a special coat, which becomes a symbol of this favoritism. Joseph's brothers (who are also infected with this sin problem) are so mad about this favoritism he receives and the lack of humility Joseph exudes that they actually sell Joseph as a slave to the Egyptians. Then, in order to deceive their father, they bring back the special coat Jacob gave Joseph, with blood on it, in order to provide false evidence that Joseph had been ravaged by a fierce animal (Genesis 37:33, ESV). When Jacob hears the news of his son's death, he is devastated. What is he supposed to believe? He could not imagine his sons would lie about such a thing as this.

As you will soon see, as this incredible story continues, God teaches us something very valuable. The most hurtful and disappointing things in our lives can be redeemed and used by God for good. It does not mean what is bad is good, but rather, even though something is bad, with God's help, good can come from it. One thing our hardships can do is build our character. This helps us to become more like Him so that we can better multiply who He is.

After Joseph was sold as a slave and taken in captivity to Egypt, he winds up in an Egyptian prison. However, God has not forgotten about him, and furthermore, God has a magnificent plan for Joseph. In fact, God ends up giving Joseph special ability while he is in this prison, the miraculous ability to interpret dreams. One time, the Pharaoh of Egypt had a dream he did not understand. Pharaoh had heard that there was this man in prison, a foreigner, named Joseph, who could interpret dreams. Joseph was summoned to Pharaoh's presence to hear the dream. And interpret it he did. The dream indicated that there was going to be seven years of prosperous crops followed by seven years of severe drought and famine. Pharaoh was wise and trusted Joseph, his dream, and Joseph's interpretation. Over the next seven years he put Joseph in charge of storing up grain so that when the drought came there would be enough food to survive the famine. Joseph so impressed Pharaoh, and God provided Joseph so much favor, that pharaoh put Joseph in charge of his kingdom, second in rank only to the pharaoh himself. After storing up grain in the years of prosperity, the drought came, and it came hard. Egypt ended up becoming the only place in the region where people could buy grain. Meanwhile, Jacob and his remaining family, back in the land where Joseph was originally from, were nearly dying of starvation. So Jacob, hearing about the grain in Egypt, with his family desperate to survive, sends his sons to Egypt to buy grain. Remember, Jacob believes his favorite son, Joseph, has been killed, and his brothers, although they had sold him, had no idea what had become of him these many years later.

Now remember that this family, the family line of Abraham, Isaac, and Jacob, is the family line of God. God had promised Abraham that his family line would multiply to be like the stars in the sky. Do you see what God did? God, knowing the famine was coming, *allowed* Joseph to be sold into slavery. God knew Joseph would become second in command to Pharaoh, and in charge of all of Egypt, so that when God's chosen family needed food, there would be a way for them to survive. God knows what He is doing!

Imagine what is about to happen next. Joseph's brothers, unknowingly, are about to see him again. Can you conceive of such a reunion? What was Joseph going to say to his brothers? What were the brothers going to say to Joseph? What were they going to have to explain to their father Jacob? When the brothers arrive in Egypt, Joseph recognizes them immediately, but they did not recognize him since he is now in this commanding position. How could they have ever thought this would be how he would end up? Although we don't have time for the complete story, it would be great to consider reading it for yourself, in Genesis chapters 37-47.

After a series of events, here is what happened when Joseph revealed himself to his brothers.

Then Joseph could not control himself before all those who stood by him. He cried, "Make everyone go out from me." So no one stayed with him when Joseph made himself known to his brothers. And he wept aloud, so that the Egyptians heard it, and the household of Pharaoh heard it. And Joseph said to his brothers, "I am Joseph! Is my father still alive?" But his bothers could not answer him, for they were dismayed at his presence.

So Joseph said to his brothers, "Come near to me, please."

And they came near. And he said,

"I am your brother Joseph, whom you sold into Egypt.

And now do not be distressed or angry with yourselves

because you sold me here, for God sent me

before you to preserve your life. For the

famine has been in the land these two years and there are yet

five years in which there will be neither plowing or harvest.

And God sent me before you to preserve you a remnant

on earth and to keep alive for you many survivors.

So it was not you who sent me here, but God."

(GENESIS 45:1-8, ESV)

Wow, what a remarkable response from Joseph! Only a man close to God could respond in such a way to such great injustice done to him by his own brothers. What great wisdom! I am sure he had to wrestle with this in order to get to this point of victory in forgiveness. There is a message in this that we cannot pass up. God can use the most painful times in your life for good if you will wrestle with Him for the wisdom and forgiveness needed to get the victory. This also displays to us that God is always working and has a plan even if we cannot see it.

So what was the purpose of sharing this entire story? Well, besides adding some light to our theme of an offering through Abraham and Isaac, this continued story of Jacob, Joseph, and the famine leads us to one of the greatest miracles of God in the history of mankind: the Passover. We can now begin to understand what set the stage for God's people needing a Passover. Jacob ends up moving his whole family to Egypt to survive the famine, and survive they did. In fact, they thrived! Pharaoh gave them the best of his land, and Jacob's family multiplied, just as God said they would. Remarkable. God is going to accomplish what He promises. He said he would multiply His people, and He did this despite a barren woman (Sarah), sinful people (all of them), and even a famine.

This famine was indeed severe and lengthy. This meant that Jacob's family still needed to buy their food from the Egyptians. Eventually, Jacob's family, the Israelites, sold all of their livestock and possessions in order to buy food to survive. It was not so bad because this particular Pharaoh had given them favor, and Joseph was still in command.

But after Joseph and this Pharaoh pass on, the future leaders of Egypt were not as kind to the Israelites. They end up treating the Israelites as slave laborers for Pharaoh's building campaign. Although Israel, God's family, has been saved from starvation and has multiplied, the people are not free. Where is this story leading? How is God going to continue to work toward a solution to reach His ultimate objective of His people being free to multiply His image and likeness in people throughout the nations?

Discussion Questions

1) Why is understanding and learning the Old Testament important to understanding the New Testament?

2) What are some of the parallels of Abraham and Isaac to the story of Jesus' sacrifice? How does the below statement of Abraham become prophetic in this story and in Jesus?

   **Abraham said, "God will provide for himself
   the lamb for a burnt offering, my son."**

   (GENESIS 22:8a)

3) How does God end up using a terrible travesty that happened to Joseph for good? Do you have examples of how God has used something bad in your life for good?

4) How does Joseph respond to his brothers when he reveals himself to them? What can we learn from him in this way? Is there a person God desires for you to forgive?

5) What ends up happening to the Israelites in Egypt?

Chapter Seven

The Passover

As slaves in Egypt, God's people cried out for freedom, and God heard their cry. What happens next is one of the greatest acts of God in the history of mankind. It also is an Old Testament arti- fact that, when we shine the light of the New Testament on it, will reveal powerful evidence, which in turn will build our faith. When you hear thunder you know there is lightning, and when we dis- cover how God weaves this all together we will know there is God.

After God hears the cries of His people, he raises up a leader named Moses to lead His people out from this bondage in Egypt. Although there is much we could say about Moses' upbringing and the many years he spent away from Egypt living in the desert among desert peoples, there is no stopping us now, so onward to the Passover event we go. God communicates to Moses that He wants Moses to go to Pharaoh and tell Pharaoh to let God's people go. You may remember the story of God telling Moses this while he watched in amazement at the burning bush that was not consumed by flame. So Moses, a man not known for eloquent speech, is asked to do the impossible. To go to the Egyptian pharaoh and tell him that God commands that this Egyptian king let the Israelites go. If God can make Moses a mouthpiece for Himself, He can do it for you too! But, it might not surprise you that Pharaoh is having none of this. Despite a couple of miracles that God gives Moses to display to Pharaoh that the message Moses gives is truly from God, Pharaoh is not buying it. God then gives Moses a series of warning messages to give to Pharaoh in regard to devastating plagues that take place in Egypt if Pharaoh will not let God's people go. Pharaoh's heart is extremely hardened, and despite these plagues, he is incredibly defiant in not changing his mind. Over the next several months God turns the River Nile to blood, infiltrates Egypt with locusts and frogs, brings a massively destructive hailstorm, kills the Egyptian livestock, and brings four other plagues for a total of nine different plagues on Pharaoh and the Egyptian people! Pharaoh had plenty of warnings, yet even after multiple warnings and successive plagues, Pharaoh remains stiff-necked. By not heeding the warnings and instruction of God through Moses, Pharaoh and Egypt are now going to experience the tenth and final plague.

The tenth plague and the events surrounding it will become known as the Passover, one of the most incredible acts of God ever recorded. In the tenth plague God is going to send a destroyer over Egypt and kill every firstborn in Egypt. Pharaoh, who has a firstborn son, will experience the full measure of this plague in his own family. God, in order to protect his people, the Israelites, gives them some very important instructions. The night that all of this is going to go down is given to the Israelites. It will be the fourteenth day of the first month on the Hebrew calendar. The month was called Nissan. For us, this is the same as either March or April, depending on the moon cycle. This will become important later. The instructions given by God begin to speak directly to our theme of offerings. God's people were instructed to take an unblemished lamb and, at twilight of that day, sacrifice that lamb as an offering. They were then told to take some of the blood of the lamb and put it on the doorposts and on the lintel (supporting beam) over the top of their doors. They were then to eat the lamb that evening. And one more important instruction was given.

> **"...you shall not break any of its bones."**
>
> (EXODUS 12:46b, ESV)

This statement will become another faith builder later. So if the Israelites followed this instruction, that night, when the destroyer would come to kill all firstborn, it would "pass over" them. If blood was found over the door of their house, all those inside the home would be saved. So, of course, after seeing nine other plagues come true, the Israelites were full of trust and a healthy measure of fear, which helped ensure they would follow this instruction. Sometimes, both trust in God and fear of the consequences of not following him are needed. In this way, a healthy fear—or, you could say, a proper respect—can protect us from harm.

That night, just as had been told, the destroying Spirit of God came and killed every firstborn in Egypt, including Pharaoh's own son. Just as they had been told, all the Israelites with blood over their doors were "passed over" and their firstborn saved. When Pharaoh saw this devastation, and felt it in his very own home, he finally, at least momentarily, had a change in heart and told Moses and the Israelites to go. The Israelites, already packed up, left Egypt to embrace this victory and freedom from many hard years of slavery and bondage. Unfortunately, Pharaoh's heart would harden once again. He chased down the Israelites and caught them from behind as the Israelites were blocked by the Red Sea. God's plan seemed doomed. But Moses was a man of great courage, and God was not going to allow His plan to be thwarted. This was truly a biblical *Braveheart* type of moment.

And Moses said to the people: *"Fear not, stand firm, and see the salvation of the Lord, which he will work for you today. For the Egyptians whom you see today, you shall never see again. The Lord will fight for you, and you have only to be silent."*

(EXODUS 14:13, 14, ESV)

Moses then stretched out his hand over the sea and the sea was held up like a wall on each side, and the Israelites miraculously walked through that sea on dry ground. Look at what happens next, when the Egyptians followed behind...

The waters returned and covered the chariots and the horseman; of all the host of Pharaoh that had followed them into the sea, not one of them remained. But the people of Israel walked on dry ground through the sea, the waters being a wall to them on their right and on their left. Thus the Lord saved Israel that day from the hand of the Egyptians, and Israel saw the Egyptians dead on the seashore. Israel saw the great power that the Lord used against the Egyptians, so the people feared the Lord, and they believed in the Lord and in his servant Moses.

(EXODUS 14:28-31, ESV)

Try as the filmmakers might, no movie can fully capture what the real thing would have been like.

This incredibly miraculous event became known as the Passover. It was never to be forgotten.

God gave special instructions that His people were to remember and celebrate this day forever, every year, on the 14th day of Nissan. Every year the Israelites were to have a feast, and each family was to sacrifice a lamb in honor of God and in memory of this special day. It became a feast that would start on the first eve of Passover and be celebrated for a week. God's people, who had multiplied in Egypt, were now finally free to establish a community where they could worship God.

Before we move on we need to highlight some points to remember.

- First, God sent His destroyer over Egypt, but through the offering of a lamb and the blood of the lamb over the door, God's people were saved.

- Second, the lamb used was to be an unblemished one.

- Third, one of the instructions God gave was that the Israelites were not to break any of the bones of the sacrificial lamb.

- Fourth, this Passover celebration was to be commemorated annually, beginning on the same day each year.

The people cried for freedom. God heard their cry and freed them from Egypt. That did not mean life would be easy. Following God can be that way. So what happens to this freed community of people? How will their newfound freedom and their historical tendency to sin mix? Despite their sin, how will God establish a way to strengthen and restore them to His image? And might He once again enjoy a relationship with them?

Discussion Questions
••••••••••••••••••••••••••••••••••••••

1) Describe with each other your general knowledge regarding the plagues in Egypt, and the stubbornness of the Egyptian pharaoh.

2) What were some of the instructions given regarding the sacrifice "offering" of the Passover Lamb?

   a. What word was used to describe its purity?

   b. What were they to do with the blood?

   c. What instruction was given regarding the lamb's bones?

3) What happened the night of this first Passover? How were the people protected from the destroying spirit? What happened next at the Red Sea?

4) What do you think God's purpose was in desiring the Israelites to be freed from Egypt? How do you think God wanted them to use that freedom? God has given us great freedom to worship him in America. How well do you think we are doing in using that freedom? What is one area you could change in order to use the freedom you have been given to worship God?

5) How did God command them to commemorate this incredible event known as the Passover?

Chapter Eight

God's Historic Offer of Atonement

We now need to enter in and imagine what the people of God will be experiencing. They had lived as a community of slaves for hundreds of years in Egypt. In a very short period of time, in haste, they grab their stuff and venture out toward freedom. In this exodus (yes, that's how the book got its name) they have no permanent shelter, they lack many basic needs, and they're without an established government. Despite God's amazing Passover miracles, when, as people, our natural needs are not met, our emotions can spill over onto ourselves. Now in the desert, trying to survive, they begin to quickly complain to their leader, Moses, about the conditions they are experiencing. They are hungry, thirsty, and, as a result, irritable. They even begin to proclaim that they were better off in Egypt where there was food and water, rather than suffering and even dying out in the desert.

Miraculously, God provides once again! He brings water from a rock, bread from the sky, and an abundance of quail from which the Israelites can eat to survive. God's people watch God provide again and again through Moses. Despite most of their physical needs now being met, this family of God's people becomes very dysfunctional. It is easy to understand why. They are without government, police, community structure, and written laws. This is a tough spot for Moses, and it leads us to an interesting story.

God calls Moses up the mountain of Mount Sinai to speak to him and begin to reveal to him what He wants Moses to write down, all in order to communicate to the people and give them some rules and guidance to live by. On the top of the mountain, God gives Moses the Ten Commandments—and a whole lot more. These instructions will end up becoming a significant portion of what is called the Books of the Law. The portion of these instructions that we are most focused on is known as the Old Testament books of Exodus and Leviticus. This was a significant amount of information given to the Israelites, and rightfully so, as it would set in stone what God's people would need to know in order to follow God and have a functioning community. One misconception readers today have about these Old Testament rules and laws is that they must have seemed so "burdensome" to God's people. Although they did end up becoming that way, it was not necessarily that way from the beginning. Imagine for a moment that although the Israelites have seen miracles of God, they do not at this point have any written instruction from Him. At this point the Old Testament was not yet written, and even if it was, they did not have a printing press. They had to wonder so much about what God was like and what He desired. Then Moses receives this information from God, and Moses is about to reveal to them God's written Word. Although they would have a hard time following it, receiving this Law would be a gift and further revelation of God to them. They could now begin to know much more about who God was and what He was like. I think we take this for granted today. The Bible is the number one best-selling book of all time, and yet many people do not care to read it to get to know God better. One of the greatest things I believe we can do with our time is to get to know God better through His Word. It is life-changing. These people were about to have this privilege.

With this being said, on one occasion, Moses, who was receiving guidance from God, was away for quite a while. This was a significant amount of instruction he was receiving from God, and so Moses was away for a period of forty days. The people back in the community didn't have a complete understanding of what was happening with Moses while he was away, and may have wondered if he is ever coming back. Without their leader, and given their previous grumbling and complaining, one can only imagine what they will do now. It didn't go well. While Moses was away, they felt the need to worship something and, instead of worshiping God directly, they made an idol of a golden calf and bowed down to worship it. God was not pleased. Imagine how He must have felt. He freed these people from Egypt, performed miracles for both their release and their provision in the desert, and now, because their spiritual leader leaves for a period of forty days, they impatiently and impulsively start worshipping some stupid, lifeless idol.

Despite this taking place long ago (about 3,500 years ago), it mirrors exactly what happens today. As we get disconnected from God, we too can mistakenly worship things in place of Him. It may be a sport or hobby, a job, money, early retirement, or simply the worship of ourselves. These things become *our* golden calves. We all worship something. It is very sinfully natural for us to worship something other than God when we forget to place our thoughts on Him and forget to remember what He has done throughout history. In order to evaluate what we worship, it is wise to consider a few questions. What is our focus? What do we spend our time on? What is the current goal that is most recognizable in our lives? God desires that our number one goal be to love Him, seek to become more like Him, and multiply Him in others. If that is not the focus of our lives, we may be worshipping a golden calf, and worse yet, not even be aware of how far off His path we have gone. As we will learn from this story, the solution is to begin to get our thoughts back on God and draw near to Him so He can realign our priorities and develop our character.

When Moses was still on the mountain with God, God could see the corruption that was taking place down in the community, and He said to Moses,

"Go down, for your people, whom you brought up out of the land of Egypt, have corrupted themselves. They have turned aside quickly out of the way I have commanded them. They have made for themselves a golden calf and have worshiped it..."

(EXODUS 32:7, 8a, ESV)

There is an interesting exchange that takes place here that I think affirms what God is after in our lives. God is so upset at His people that he tells Moses He is about to let His wrath burn hot against them. Moses then appeals to God on behalf of his people. Listen in to Moses's closing argument to God.

Moses says, "Remember Abraham, Isaac, and Israel, your servants, to whom you swore by your own self and said to them, 'I will multiply your offspring as the stars of heaven...'"

(EXODUS 32:13a)

In this statement to God he emphasizes to God the Creator's own promise and His mission! Moses essentially says the following: "God, based on the promise you made to them and the mission you called them to live out in multiplying a family of people, please turn away your wrath."

God heard these words and He relented from the punishment

He had in mind. However, Moses too was very upset, and when he returned to the Israelite camp he boldly called the people and forced them to make a definite decision. Here is what he said.

"Who is on the Lord's side? Come to me."

(EXODUS 32:26a, ESV)

Make up your mind. Who is with me and who is with God? Make a decision! Many joined him, but those who did not lost their lives. Over a thousand people who worshipped the golden calf and did not come to the Lord's side lost their lives that day. Today, there is a very true concept and teaching that God is love. In fact, the Bible affirms this, and simply so.

"...God is love."

(1 JOHN 4:8a, ESV)

However, He is not only love. God is not who we want to make Him to be. He is who He is, and if you read the Bible, His actions do not demonstrate that He is a one-sided coin called love. That is a misconception about God. Man has a sin problem, and when Adam and Eve sinned, He kicked them out of the garden. When the world became wicked, He flooded the earth. When Sodom and Gomorrah became utterly sinful, He destroyed the city and all of its inhabitants. When people worshipped the golden calf, He was angry and many people lost their lives. Sometimes we need to say it clearly, like Moses did.

"Who is on the Lord's side? Come to me."

(EXODUS 32:26a, ESV)

Are you on the Lord's side? I hope many readers of this book will choose to be on the Lord's side or, if believers, to become more steadfast in faith to stay on the Lord's side. That is the purpose of this book. God uses many means to convince us to take these steps. Miracles, evidence recorded in the Scriptures, God's love, God's grace, His forgiveness, and at times things He has done and said that gives us some awe, reverential respect, and fear for His name. All of these aspects of God work together to help us choose to be on His side. He goes through great pains to get us to follow Him.

Now we will move on to discover an example of the grace of God. As we go on, this will continue to be revealed in a grand way.

Forgiveness through Atonement

God now does something that displays His love, His great grace, and His desire to be in fellowship with them, and with us, despite our sinful tendencies. God's response to the golden calf debacle was not wrath, but rather a plan to restore His people to Himself. Ever since the garden, man has proven to have a strong tendency to sin, and that sin separates us from a close relationship with God. That separation tends to make things even worse because when we are not close with God our sin increases all the more. We can see this in our own lives. The more distant we are from God the more we sin, and the more distant we then become. How will He restore us to relationship with Him despite our sin? At this point in history He foreshadows what will later become a grand fulfillment. The following story will help us prepare to understand what the people's relationship to God was like after the golden calf incident, and show us God's ultimate response to that sin.

Imagine for a moment a husband and wife are separated and perhaps even contemplating divorce. They are not spending time together and no longer live in the same house. Perhaps sin got in the way to divide them. In this case the husband cheated, much like the Israelites did through their golden calf. The wife is having a hard time moving past this sin. She may even be feeling a sense of wrath! However, in this case, and pleasantly, the husband is repentant. He is filled with sorrow. He wants his wife back. She senses his realness, the depth of his sorrow, and with God's help, she finds the strength and grace to forgive. Her husband at this point is not aware of her change of heart. He is broken, longing for her return. She calls him to set up a meeting. His anxiety has his insides churning, and his mind is utterly exasperated. When they come together again to talk, she immediately embraces him and proclaims her forgiveness for him. He doesn't know what to make of it. He is nervously excited. He almost can't believe it. Is this real? Does she mean this? Oh, how he hopes so, but he is scared. Perhaps she is just emotional. She then says something that irons her decision into his soul. She tells him that she wants to start over and even build a new home together. She wants to start fresh and plan together for the future. This is such good news to him that it almost seems reckless. He cannot believe his ears. She is saying something that has a plan involved. It is something that demonstrates that this is not just a temporary decision, but a permanent one.

This story illustrates well what God is about to do, and it may surprise you. God's relationship with the common man at this point was way more distant than it was when He started with Adam and Eve in the garden. After the golden calf incident, God, who could have responded with only wrath instead, chooses to come nearer to His people than He has in a long, long time. Since God and sin do not mix, He was about to make a way to atone for their sin so they could be in a right relationship again. God essentially went to His bride, right after she had just cheated, and said, "I want you to build me a house where my presence can dwell right in your midst." This beautiful dwelling place of God was to be called the tabernacle. That's what *tabernacle* means: a dwelling place, and in this case a dwelling place for God. When Moses told the people that God wanted them to build this tabernacle, they were overjoyed. But this is not really surprising. I envision them being so repentant from their collective golden calf behavior that when God essentially said He wanted them to partner with Him, to build a place where His presence would dwell in their midst, they responded with overwhelming gratefulness for the grace and mercy of God.

We can see evidence that this was exactly how they felt by what happens next. When Moses, on behalf of God, asks them to bring together supplies and donate their skills and services to build this dwelling place for God, they respond by bringing so much that Moses has to tell them to stop. Seriously! As a pastor, I can assure you every church would love to have this problem!

Much like the story of Abraham and Isaac, the tabernacle foreshadows much of what is to be later fulfilled. Although there is so much more that could be revealed about this tabernacle, we will underscore a few important aspects for the purpose of continuing to reveal the significance of an offering.

On the outside of the tabernacle all of God's people camped. They were told to live in tents, literally, all around the tabernacle in order to keep God's dwelling place in their sight. It is true that when man keeps God in the forefront of his mind, man is better at following God. God's people had such a hard time following Him that God came up with a solution, a way of staying in their midst.

The tabernacle had only one entrance gate. An Israelite male could enter the gate with his offering to God. Someone not of the family of God's people could bring an offering to God, but that person would not be able to enter the gate. Once inside the gate, there is what is called the courtyard. There, sacrifices would be made, and other items existed such as an altar for the sacrifice and a basin to wash in. Within this walled-in area there was, on the opposite end, a tent structure that was the true tabernacle. Only the priests could enter this portion of the tabernacle. This tent had two chambers; the first was called the Holy Place; the second, more inner, chamber, which was separated by a thick veil, was called the Most Holy Place. Only the priests could enter the Holy Place, and only the high priest could enter the Most Holy Place and only on one day per year, what was known as the Day of Atonement. This was a special day when the high priest would make a sacrificial offering on behalf of the whole community. Inside the Most Holy Place was the Ark of the Covenant, and the presence of God Himself. Above this Most Holy Place a pillar of smoke would demonstrate to the people camped outside the tabernacle that God's presence was with them. God, who was present with Adam and Eve in the garden, is now present in the tabernacle.

Below, you see a diagram of the tabernacle.

We are now ready to get to a central theme of utmost importance in the message of this book. When an Israelite would sin, he was instructed by one of the Books of the Law (Leviticus) to bring an offering to the entrance of the tabernacle in order for his sin to be atoned for. Like the Passover lamb, the offering was usually a lamb or goat, and the animal was to be unblemished. An unblemished animal would be of highest value; God was desiring we would bring our very best sacrificial offering. Through history we have learned that the lamb would be inspected by the priests to ensure that the lamb was indeed unblemished. It is even possible that the lamb was marked with some sort of seal to indicate that the animal had passed inspection.[2] This was done in Egypt, and the Jewish people may have followed this practice. This could be important when many sacrifices were being made, to ensure that no one substituted a blemished animal for an unblemished one. When it was found to be unblemished, the sacrifice could then take place. Here were the instructions given on the sacrificial procedure:

> **"...the sin which he has committed is made known to him,**
> **he shall bring as his offering a goat, a male without blemish,**
> **and shall lay his hand on the head of the goat and kill it in the**
> **place where they kill the burnt offering before the Lord,**
> **it is a sin offering. Then the priest shall take**
> **some of the blood of the sin offering**
> **put it on the horns of the altar... So the priest shall make**
> **atonement for him for his sin, and he shall be forgiven."**
>
> (LEVITICUS 4:23-26, ESV)

Imagine this scene as though it involved *you*. You have sinned and you know this sin is getting in the way of a right relationship between you and God. You know that God desires a relationship with you and has made a way to atone for your sin. You look forward to being forgiven and being in right standing with God. You choose from your animals your very best sacrifice, an unblemished lamb or goat, and you walk your lamb to the tabernacle entrance gate. When arriving, the priest inspects your lamb by walking around it and looking for blemishes. You are relieved that yours is found to be unblemished, and it is sealed. You then are permitted inside the gate with your lamb. You are now on holy ground. The priest has you lay one hand on the lamb. You can feel a lamb's chest move as it breaths. You then are given a knife to slice the throat of the lamb. Yes, I want you to envision this. This may seem foreign to you, but it was not to that culture. In a culture without refrigeration, if you wanted to eat meat you learned how to sacrifice an animal. So there you stand in the tabernacle with your hand on the animal and a knife made ready for blood that is about to be shed. So you do what you came to do and you feel the lamb die under your hand. It is a bloody scene. The blood shed is the evidence that the animal's life was taken. The life is in the blood of the animal. The priest then takes the lamb and places the lamb on the altar of God. He then takes some of the blood and sprinkles it over the altar. You have honored God. Your sin has now been atoned for. The sin that was on you has been atoned for and the penalty for that sin was placed on the lamb. The lamb was your substitute. God, as demonstrated through Cain and Abel, Noah, Abraham and Isaac, the Passover lamb, and now this tabernacle lamb, shows that He is pleased with a sacrificial offering. Through that offering and the shedding of blood, He forgives sin and saves His people. He saved His people through the blood of a lamb at Passover, he gave Abraham a substitutional sacrifice rather than the boy Isaac, and now here at the tabernacle God's means for restoring a relationship to Him is made apparent through the offering of the blood of a lamb. You now leave the temple court, and the priest either burns the offering or, many times, uses it for food.

God made a way to restore proper standing before Him, and it feels good to be reconciled when one was previously divided. Forgiveness has been obtained...at least temporarily. When a person would sin, their required course of action would be the same; they would need to bring a sacrificial offering again. Now if you were in this situation, I think it is safe to say you might be less likely to choose to sin, knowing that if you did, this would all have to be repeated. Keep in mind that these animals were valuable, and you would not want to continue to lose their value unnecessarily.

Despite this method of atonement, God's people continue to struggle with following Him. The regular sacrifices were meant to be a reminder to honor Him and put God first. Over the next hundreds of years, God's people are unfaithful in a number of ways in regards to this sacrificial means of atonement. The mistakes they make in this regard are varied. One example is that they completely disregard God and do not even bother bringing Him a sacrifice. Essentially, they forget or ignore His desire for them to bring Him an offering. Many in our world today are in this same boat. They forget about God and discontinue seeking Him and stop attending church. Many, either because of disbelief of the Bible or because of the separation they are experiencing in their relationship with God, stop reading their Bibles. As a result, their relationship with God is distant and they are much less likely to follow His ways.

The second problem that the Israelites faced was bringing their sacrifice as a rule, or obligation, rather than doing it because of their love for God and their desire to be restored to a right relationship with Him. This could be compared today to people who go to church, but when they are there, they are simply going through the motions. Examples of this could be not focusing on what is being presented, texting, checking Facebook, essentially being physically present but mentally absent. That person may be at church, but he or she is hardly paying attention, not really seeking to apply what is being said, but rather simply checking church off the list. In America, people drive to the right of the center line on the way to church, but when they leave many no longer think much about having a life that lines up with God. God's people in Moses' day were similar, and as a result God grew frustrated with their meaningless sacrifices. It is not that the sacrificial offering was not something God desired, it's that what makes it right is a right heart. In the same way our attendance at church is so much more valuable when our hearts are engaged in wanting to grow closer to God.

In the story of God's people, the Israelites now go through a long season of yo-yoing with God. At times they would follow Him, and then they would fall right back into the same sinful habits. This pattern lasted for more than a thousand years.

During this time frame God raised up prophet after prophet to speak on His behalf, letting His people know He was not impressed with their sacrifices when their hearts were far from Him.

"What to me is the multitude of your sacrifices?" says the Lord; "I have enough of burnt offerings of rams and the fat of well-fed beasts; I do not delight in the blood of bulls, or of lambs, or of goats. When you come to appear before me, who has required of you this trampling of my courts? Bring no more vain offerings;..."

(ISAIAH 1:11-13a, ESV)

In sacrifice and offering you have not delighted, but you have given me an open ear. Burnt offering and sin offering you have not required. Then I said, "Behold, I have come; in the scroll of the book it is written of me. I delight to do your will, O my God; your law is within my heart."

(PSALM 40:6-8, ESV)

So the question becomes: what is God going to do about this condition? Fortunately, the plan is no longer that of starting completely over, as in the days of Noah. The story of this book and the story of God is how He consistently and patiently works with sinful people to achieve His original objective of multiplying His image and likeness in people throughout the nations. God's people seem to be in a perpetual cycle of falling away from Him. How is God going to break this cycle, and how will He follow His long-established pattern of using a sacrifice to do it? God's prophets had much more to say about God's frustration with the meaningless sacrifices of the people. God was beginning to reveal to them what one day would come.

When one walks from one end of a playground teeter-totter to another, there is a point that is reached where momentum builds and the teeter-totter powerfully rushes to the ground on the other side. We are nearing that point. In the next critical chapter of this book, several more ancient artifacts will be dug up, and then shortly after that we will brush them off to discover diamonds of faith.

Congratulations on continuing along with the journey to this point. Thus far in this book, we have been lacing one side of the shoe. Soon the other lace will appear, and we will tie a knot of faith.

Discussion Questions

1) What happened with the people when Moses was away on the mountain?

2) What choice was given to the people when Moses returned? How does this relate to the choice of faith we must make today?

3) Describe the tabernacle and how God's presence came near.

4) Given all the disobedience of God's people to this point, how was the tabernacle an act of grace on God's part?

5) How did people receive atonement at the tabernacle?

6) Briefly recall all of the different offerings we have seen to date.

   a. Cain and Abel

   b. Noah

   c. Abraham and Isaac

   d. Passover

   e. Tabernacle

7) How do you think people ended up dishonoring God in their offerings to Him? What could Isaiah have meant by Isaiah 1:11-13?

8) How could we be compared to the Israelites in dishonoring God today in our "religious" church involvement? What is the difference between doing something (like going to church) simply to say that we did it, compared with doing something from the heart?

Chapter Nine

Prophecy: What Do the Dead Sea Scrolls Have to Do with It?

So far we have followed the journey of God's people from when they were removed from the garden, to starting over with Noah after the flood, to the mass exodus from Egypt through the miracle of the Passover and Passover lamb, and finally, the grace of God exhibited after the golden calf incident. This was done by providing a place of atonement through the offering of a lamb at God's tabernacle. This breadth of biblical history is important and will inspire people to faith when the light of the New Testament is cast upon it.

Through this entire book we have been laying a foundation. This chapter is the final one in that regard: the building of the foundation. When the foundation is ready and the lumber is on site, this building of faith will pop up rather quickly. That stage of building is always very exciting! We will now make the final and important preparations for that stage.

In the timeline of history, when the Israelites get to the tabernacle of God in the desert, it was approximately the 1440s B.C. That is the season God began to give His people what is known as the Law, or the Books of the Law. These books, the first five books of the Bible, written by Moses, are considered the Mosaic Law. Another name for these books that you may have heard is the Torah. Essentially, these names are synonymous for what are the books of Genesis, Exodus, Leviticus, Numbers, and Deuteronomy. These books make up the very important first section of the Old Testament. The Old Testament is also known as the Old Covenant. Another way of saying covenant would be to say agreement. When speaking of the Bible, dictionary.com defines the Old Covenant in this way:

Old Covenant: the agreement between God and the ancient Israelites, in which God promised to protect them if they kept His law and were faithful to Him.[3]

We won't take the time to go into significant detail, but it's important to know that God, in the Old Testament, makes a covenant with God's people, and they willingly agree to it. That covenant says that if they follow God they will be blessed, but if they turn away from following Him they will be cursed. In the Bible, covenants were nearly always made with blood as a means of sealing, or ratifying, the covenant. When God made what is known as the Mosaic Covenant described above, as we will see below, it was sealed with blood.

And he sent young men of the people of Israel, who offered burnt offerings and sacrificed peace offerings of oxen to the Lord. And Moses took half of the blood and put it in basins, and half of the blood he threw against the altar. Then he took the book of the covenant and read it in the hearing of the people. And they said, "All that the Lord has spoken we will do, and we will be obedient. And Moses took the blood and threw it

on the people and said, "Behold the blood of the covenant that
the Lord has made with you in accordance with all these words."

(EXODUS 24:5-8, ESV)

Sadly, as we have shown throughout this book, God's people
are not good on their word. Mankind, who has inherited a sin
problem from Adam, has a very difficult time being consistently
faithful to God and His covenant. In fact, we can safely say that
over the next 1,400 years, God's people live in a continuous cycle
of falling away from God, being disciplined for it, returning to God,
and being restored to a beautiful relationship with Him, only to
later then fall away from Him again—and this cycle would repeat
over and over. In this season of time, when God's people had great
leadership, they would rid the community of idols and return to
worshipping God. When there was poor leadership, they would
essentially go back to worshipping whatever was their golden calf
of the moment. One of the problems at the heart of their falling
away was not remembering, or not fixing their thoughts on, what
God had done and said. In fact, on one occasion, for a long period
of time, the people of God actually forgot about and literally lost
the Books of the Law in the temple treasury. When a good Israelite king, named Josiah, found their Bible, he immediately repented
and read it in the hearing of the people so they could remember all
that God had done and said (see 2 Kings chapters 22, 23).

Today, it is so very important that we get grounded in a full understanding of all that God has done and said and reflect deeply on
the evidence that has been left behind so that we can be strengthened in our resolve to follow Him. That is a significant purpose of
this book. This evidence woven through the Scriptures provides for
us God's miracles on display. Although I cannot show you the miracle of the Passover in person, I can illustrate the miracles of God
fulfilling His Word. Sometimes it's as though people of the world
think: why does God not just do a miracle for us? Is that fair? Do

we all personally need to see a miracle like the Passover with our own eyes to believe and follow God? Should God have to perform a miracle for each and every person, of each and every generation, in order for us to believe? Where would faith come in if that were necessary? But that does not mean our faith is without evidence. There indeed is significant evidence that, once we've learned it, can help us build a strong fire of faith. Let's lay out the remaining artifacts for inspection now.

During this 1,400-year season of history, God raises up many prophets to speak on his behalf. These are guys you likely have heard of—Isaiah, Micah, Jeremiah, Joel, and many more—to whom God pours words (prophecy) into their hearts and minds in order that they may speak to both warn and encourage God's people to follow Him. Another form of prophecy is when God gave them words to share and write down about something that was going to take place in the future. Some of the things they predicted (prophesied about) happened shortly thereafter. Other prophecies that were given were to be fulfilled at a later date. Many of these prophecies are about a person who would come from God in the future to restore people back to God and build God's Kingdom. These prophecies called this person, who was to come, by a variety of names, including Messiah, King, Immanuel, Prince, Servant, and others. They also foretold many things about this Messiah's birth, life, and death. What is incredible, as you will soon see, is that these prophecies came true. In fact, these prophecies were fulfilled so closely to what was spoken that many skeptics had a hard time believing it was possible. They believed there had to be some kind of explanation, other than a miracle from God, for how this could occur.

One explanation given, which could be viewed as somewhat difficult to refute, is this: how could we be certain that the prophecy truly predated the fulfillment? Allow me to explain. One of the problems Christians had in proving these prophetic fulfillments was that a copy of the prophetic text, one older than the fulfillment, did not exist. After all, it is difficult to preserve a scroll from 700 B.C. to prove that it was indeed written prior to the fulfillment of events that took place from 1 B.C. to 33 A.D. Now, Christians, and many scientists, still believed that the prophecies were given prior to the events being fulfilled, but they did not have an actual, historically dated copy of the text to prove it. One of the reasons we still believed the prophecies were older than the fulfillment of them, however, was from what is considered textual evidence. Let me provide a modern example of this in layman's terms. It is believed that the word *dude* originated from the song "Yankee Doodle Dandy" from the late 1700s. The doodle part at first was shortened to "dood," and then became dude in the late 1800s. It was the description of a Yankee (Northerner) who was trying to look sharply dressed.[4]

So to give you one example of textual evidence, if a person was trying to date some written material and the word *dude* was used, one would know that it most likely had to be written in the late 1800s or later. In a similar way, people of yesteryear wrote with words and style that marked the era they lived in. So through the comparison of other materials written from those eras, one can make educated judgments about when something was written. Another form of textual evidence comes when one writes and mentions events that had taken place in their day, or the fact that key events that did take place are not mentioned. If an event is mentioned, then one can know the author must have written it after that event. If you know the time of the event, you then gain evidence to when it was written. As an example, if a book mentions what occurred on 9/11 (the September 2011 terrorist attacks in America), one would know the book had to be written after that date. So, based on this type of evidence, and other forms not mentioned, it was always believed that Old

Testament books were indeed old, but we still did not have a copy that would give significantly further proof. In fact, the oldest copies of the Old Testament that scholars had were from the ninth and tenth centuries A.D. That makes them a thousand or more years old today (a very old piece of paper!), but still way off the mark in terms of being before the key events that took place from 1 B.C. to 33 A.D. that we will soon be focusing on. Below is a timeline to help make sense of this.

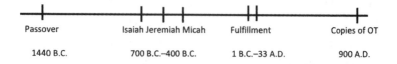

Passover	Isaiah Jeremiah Micah	Fulfillment	Copies of OT
1440 B.C.	700 B.C.–400 B.C.	1 B.C.–33 A.D.	900 A.D.

So the prophecies written throughout history, and in particular what the prophets wrote between 700 to 400 B.C., did not last in a preserved form for easy proof that they were written prior to the fulfillment of their words, which came from 1 B.C. to 33 A.D. I don't believe it was ever thought that a copy that predated the events of 1 B.C.–33 A.D. would ever be found, or that a copy of a text that old still existed on planet earth...but God. Have you ever heard that expression before? "But God." It is used in such a way that describes the impossible, at least the impossible for anybody "but God." Not long ago an amazing discovery took place that is a "but God" moment for us today. With Him all things are possible. Here is the story of how the Dead Sea Scrolls were found.

Juma was beginning to get nervous. Some of his goats were climbing too high up the cliffs. He decided to climb the face of the cliff himself to bring them back. Little did Juma realize as he began his climb on that January day in 1947 that those straying goats would eventually involve him in "the greatest archaeological discovery in the twentieth century." Such thoughts were far from his mind when he saw two small openings to one of the thousands of caves that dot those barren cliffs overlooking the northwestern shore of the Dead Sea.

He threw a rock into one of the openings. The unexpected cracking sound surprised him; what else could be in those remote caves but treasure? He called to his cousins, Khalil and Muhammed, who climbed up and heard the exciting tale. But it was getting late, and the goats had to be gathered. Tomorrow they would return—perhaps their days of following goats would come to an end once the treasure was uncovered!

The youngest of the three, Muhammed, rose the next day before his two fellow "treasure seekers" and made his way to the cave. The cave floor was covered with debris, including broken pottery. Along the wall stood a number of narrow jars, some with their bowl-shaped covers still in place. Frantically, Muhammed began to explore the inside of each jar, but no treasure of gold was to be found...[there were] only a few bundles wrapped in cloth and greenish with age. Returning to his cousins, he related the sad news—no treasure.

No treasure indeed! The scrolls those Bedouin boys removed from that dark cave that day and the days following would come to be recognized as the greatest manuscript treasure ever found—the first seven manuscripts of the Dead Sea Scrolls![5]

The Dead Sea Scrolls were copies of the Old Testament and other materials a group of people living in that region had likely preserved during a season of persecution. They are called the Dead Sea Scrolls simply because they were found in caves in the Dead Sea area. What Juma and Muhammed did not know when they found the first copies was that the group of people who lived in the many caves in this region of the Dead Sea—around

100 B.C.—had a massive, historic library cavern of these scrolls that had remained hidden and preserved all these years. In the years to come, thousands of scrolls were discovered in these caves. Truly, and totally, incredible.

These Old Testament scrolls were scientifically dated and were found to be from 100–300 B.C., significantly older than the fulfillment of the prophecies, which came, as we said, from 1 B.C. to 33 A.D. Let's take a look at the graph again, below, now including the discovery of the Dead Sea Scrolls.

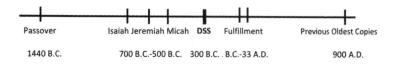

Passover	Isaiah Jeremiah Micah	DSS	Fulfillment	Previous Oldest Copies
1440 B.C.	700 B.C.-500 B.C.	300 B.C.	B.C.-33 A.D.	900 A.D.

This is significant because now we can prove that the prophecies, which we will now look at, about the One (the Messiah) who was to come, indeed predated his coming. In fact, in those caves, portions of every book of the Old Testament were found, except for the book of Esther, which is not part of the prophetic history we are covering. This point cannot be overstated. We now know, without a shadow of a doubt, that these prophetic scrolls predated what they so articulately predicted would occur. As you will see, it would be impossible to predict what they foretold…"but God."

There are literally hundreds of prophecies that have been fulfilled in the Bible. We are going to uncover some of the most powerful specific prophecies that help develop the message of this book and fan our faith into flames. I plead with you to read the Scriptures that will now be put on display. Although the full meaning will be revealed in the following chapters, it is important we are familiar with them so that when the fulfillment is shown, what has taken place can be clearly seen. Many people today think reading the Bible is boring. I would argue it is due to a lack of trust and faith. Scripture goes from dull to fascinating when one begins to see that God is the author, and that He proves what He writes through fulfilling what was spoken long ago.

In the first prophecy we hear from Micah, who ministered around the year 750 B.C. In his prophecy we learn where this King, who was predicted to come, would be born, which also hints to his lineage.

> But you, O <u>Bethlehem</u> Ephrathah,
> who are too little to be among the clans of Judah,
> <u>from you shall come forth for me</u>
> <u>one who is to be ruler in Israel,</u>
> <u>whose coming forth is from of old,</u>
> <u>from ancient days.</u>
> Therefore he shall give them up until the time
> <u>when she who is in labor has given birth;</u>
> then the rest of his brothers shall return
> to the people of Israel.
> And he shall stand and shepherd his flock
> in the strength of the LORD,
> in the majesty of the name of the LORD his God.
> And they shall dwell secure, for now he shall be great
> to the ends of the earth.
> And he shall be their peace.
>
> (MICAH 5:2-5a, ESV)

The prophecy above we learn that out of Bethlehem this ruler was to come. It was also prophesied that this King would come from the family line of David, and that David's family would have the throne forever. We learn in the Bible that David's father Jesse was from Bethlehem, making Bethlehem David's hometown. There is so much that is incredible about this story, but for the sake of our purposes here, we have learned that this Messiah to come would come from Bethlehem, the town of David.

Isaiah: 700 B.C.

We will be looking at several passages from the book of Isaiah. Isaiah lived about 700 B.C. In this verse it is foretold that we would be given the sign of a son, born of a virgin, and that His name would be called Immanuel. Immanuel means: "God with us" or "with us God."

> **Therefore the Lord himself will give you a sign.**
>
> **Behold, the virgin shall conceive and bear a son,**
>
> **and shall call his name Immanuel.**
>
> (ISAIAH 7:14, ESV)

Very interesting. From this virgin birth we are told we will receive a son who literally will be *God with us*. In the prophecy we look at next we get some very important information. We learn that He shall be a child, a son, a God, from the family line of David, and we also discover some other great titles and positions He will hold.

> **For to us a child is born, to us a son is given;and the government**
>
> **shall be upon his shoulder,and his name shall be called Wonderful**
>
> **Counselor, Mighty God,Everlasting Father, Prince of Peace.**
>
> **Of the increase of his government and of peace**
>
> **there will be no end, on the throne of David and over his kingdom,**
>
> **to establish it and to uphold it with justice and with righteousness**
>
> **from this time forth and forevermore.**
>
> **The zeal of the LORD of hosts will do this.**
>
> (ISAIAH 9:6, 7, ESV)

The next passage we will look at is perhaps the most important, profound, and amazingly accurate of all prophecies later to be fulfilled. This chapter is so good that I am going to provide the entire thing! One could literally underline the entire chapter to point out fulfillments that will come later, but I will underline several key sections for our recollection later.

Who has believed what he has heard from us? And to whom has the arm of the LORD been revealed? For he grew up before him like a young plant, and like a root out of dry ground;

he had no form or majesty that we should look at him,
and no beauty that we should desire him.
He was despised and rejected by men;
a man of sorrows, and acquainted with grief;

and as one from whom men hide their
faces he was despised, and we esteemed him not.

Surely he has borne our griefs and carried our sorrows;
yet we esteemed him stricken, smitten by God,
and afflicted. But he was pierced for our transgressions;
he was crushed for our iniquities; upon him
was the chastisement that brought us peace,
and with his wounds we are healed.
All we like sheep have gone astray;
we have turned—every one—to his own way;
and the LORD has laid on him the iniquity of us all.
He was oppressed, and he was afflicted, yet he opened not his
mouth; like a lamb that is led to the slaughter,
and like a sheep that before its shearers is silent,
so he opened not his mouth.
By oppression and judgment he was taken away;

and as for his generation, who considered that

he was cut off out of the land of the living,

stricken for the transgression of my people?

And they made his <u>grave with the wicked and with a rich</u>

<u>man in his death,</u> although he had done no violence,

and there was no deceit in his mouth.

Yet it was the will of the LORD to crush him;

he has put him to grief;

when <u>his soul makes an offering for guilt,</u>

he shall see his offspring; he shall prolong his days;

the will of the LORD shall prosper in his hand.

Out of the anguish of his soul he shall see and be satisfied;

by his knowledge shall the righteous one,

my servant, make many to be accounted righteous,

and he shall bear their iniquities.

Therefore I will divide him a portion with the many,

and he shall divide the spoil with the strong,

because he poured out his soul to death

and was numbered with the transgressors;

yet <u>he bore the sin of many,</u>

<u>and makes intercession for the transgressors.</u>

(ISAIAH 53, ESV)

There is so much there that will later be displayed. Since you have been with this book from the beginning, perhaps you notice the mention of a *lamb*? That will be significant. It is so very cool that when one reads about the Dead Sea Scrolls, they discover that this scroll from Isaiah—and more importantly, Isaiah 53—was well preserved.[6]

After Isaiah we get a prophet named Jeremiah, and he provides us with a gem of a prophecy. Previously in this chapter, I explained what is meant by the Old Testament, or Old Agreement. What Jeremiah begins to tell us (he lived about 600 B.C.) is that God will one day make a New Covenant, or New Agreement, with His people. Let's see what Jeremiah writes for us about this New Agreement.

The New Covenant

"Behold, the days are coming," declares the LORD,

"when I will make a new covenant with the house of Israel

and the house of Judah, not like the covenant that I made with

their fathers on the day when I took them by the hand to bring

them out of the land of Egypt, my covenant that they broke,

though I was their husband, declares the LORD.

For this is the covenant that I will make with the

house of Israel after those days," declares the LORD:

"I will put my law within them, and I will write it on their hearts.

And I will be their God, and they shall be my people.

And no longer shall each one teach his neighbor

and each his brother, saying, 'Know the LORD,'

for they shall all know me, from the least of them to

the greatest, declares the LORD.

For I will forgive their iniquity,

and I will remember their sin no more."

(JEREMIAH 31: 31-34 ESV)

This New Covenant sounds amazing! We all not only want, but need—and are incredibly blessed by—our sins not only being forgiven but remembered no more! Soon we will see how this New Covenant was ratified and sealed, just as was demonstrated in the Old Covenant. The last prophecy we will uncover, which will lead to an astonishing fulfillment, comes from the prophet Joel, and was given around 500 B.C.

The sun shall be turned to darkness, and the moon to blood,

before the great and awesome day of the LORD comes.

And it shall come to pass that everyone who calls

on the name of the LORD shall be saved.

(JOEL 2:31-32a)

This is so far out there that only a true and powerful God could possibly make this come true.

We have now completed our exploration of the Old Testament and have lifted some excellent artifacts from the Dead Sea caves. The dust is still on them and their complete meaning has not yet been revealed. We will now close this section by going back to our story about Juma and his discovery of the Dead Sea Scrolls. Juma was looking for a treasure. He found one that was so much more precious than the gold he was looking for. The problem is that he did not know it. Juma, not knowing what he had in these scrolls, mistakenly sold them to a local dealer.[7] That dealer too, not knowing what he had, also sold them inexpensively. They had something of both great intrinsic and huge monetary value, the oldest biblical scrolls known to mankind, but because they did not understand the value of what they had, they did not receive the full value. So an important question lies in the midst of all this: how much do you value the Word of God? Have you, possibly, like Juma, not fully known its worth, and therefore not received its full value in your life? Unlike our Babe Ruth card analogy mentioned earlier, this question matters for eternity.

Discussion Questions

1) How would you describe the Old "Mosaic" Covenant? (See Deuteronomy 11:26-28.) How was it originally ratified? (See Exodus 24:3-8.)

2) How would you describe, generally, an Old Testament "prophecy"?

3) What are the Dead Sea Scrolls and what is their significance, especially as it relates to Old Testament prophecy?

4) Who prophesied about the New Covenant? When was it prophesied? How was the New Covenant described?

5) The chapter closes with the story of Juma's discovery. Unfortunately, because Juma did not know the value of the scrolls, he sold them quickly and did not receive their full value. How does the value we place on the Scriptures impact the value we receive from them?

6) How have you seen this play out in your life and in the lives of people around you (do not name people individually!) from both a positive and negative standpoint?

Chapter Ten

The Astronomical Baby Shower

The Old Testament foretold that this day would come, but it was a long time in coming. What was envisioned long ago by the prophets was about to appear. We now know, due to the evidence of the Dead Sea Scrolls, that prophecies about Jesus' coming predated His arrival.

We are now going fast forward from the prophets to the arrival of our Lord. Many of you may remember that in the days of Jesus' birth, there was said to be an appearance of a star in the sky, one which indicated to some wise men that the birth of a King had taken place, or was about to take place. Here are some excellent questions: What took place in the sky that so captured the attention of a few important and wise people that they would travel a great distance to follow a star? Why would a single star (bright and luminous as it may be) indicate to them a King was to be born? And finally, why did they look for this King in the small Israelite town of Bethlehem?

In this section we will be taking a significant look at some astronomical research in order to discover whether there were any special happenings in the galaxy that took place that may then help us date the year of Christ's birth. Not only is it interesting to attempt to nail down the birth year of Christ, but this year becomes important in correctly discerning the year of His death on a cross. What is amazing is that when we properly discern the correct year, day, and even hour of his death, we find that some amazing activities occur in the galaxy, events that reveal God working in an incredible, predetermined fashion. These revelations will help build our faith. So we now move forward from the prophecies of 700–400 B.C. discussed in the previous chapter to the year 2 B.C.!

You may wonder: why 2 B.C.? To begin, we must first clear up a common misunderstanding regarding the terms B.C. and A.D. As an added bonus, this may one day help you look smart with friends! B.C. is an abbreviation for before Christ, a fact that many know, but A.D. does not stand for after death, which many believe. Since Jesus lived for thirty-plus years, that would leave a gap in the dating system from His birth to His death. A.D. actually stands for *anno Domini*, which means the "year of our Lord," or the year of the birth of Christ. Did you know that the world's yearly dating system is actually based on the birth of Jesus Christ?

Even though much of the world does not yet believe in Him, the world's calendar is dated by Him!

This dating system was developed in 500 A.D. At that time the people dating the calendar went back to try to determine the "year of our Lord," and from their determination our dating system was developed. Although they got close, it is now believed that the date and year determined was in error. Although the actual date of birth may never be known, evidence has been gathered that can help us discern the year. I believe the best theory of dating the year of the Lord is between 2 and 1 B.C. I'll now discuss the evidence as to why I, and many others, affirm this date.

The Bible tells us that Jesus was about thirty years old when he stepped into public ministry.

Jesus, when he began his ministry,

was about thirty years of age,

being the son (as was supposed) of Joseph ...

(LUKE 3:23, ESV)

This would then mean that if Jesus was about thirty years of age when He began His ministry, and we take the date of 2–1 B.C. for His birth, then the year His ministry started would be around 29 or 30 A.D. (Keep in mind that in this dating system there is no year 0.) So the years would move forward as follows: 2 B.C., 1 B.C., 1 A.D., 2 A.D., and so forth. We know through studying the Gospels (Matthew, Mark, Luke, and John) that the Bible mentions Jesus and His disciples acknowledging three distinct Passovers during His time of ministry. As mentioned earlier—and as will be significant for us later—the Passover was a special one-day-per-year holiday commemorating the day the blood of the lamb protected God's people and helped them escape Egypt. Through the record of Jesus observing three Passovers, we then can date the length of Jesus' ministry to just over three years. So then, if Jesus was born around the turn of 2, or 1, B.C., and began His ministry in 29–30 A.D., and He then observed three Passovers before dying in 33 A.D. (as I will later show), all of this would line up with Luke's account of Jesus starting His ministry when He was about thirty years old. The next graph may help illustrate this a bit more clearly.

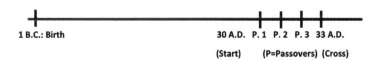

1 B.C.: Birth   30 A.D. P. 1 P. 2 P. 3 33 A.D.

                                 (Start)   (P=Passovers) (Cross)

Before we get into some astronomy, there is historical evidence to first consider. The Bible mentions that at the time of Jesus' birth there was a king named Herod. Not long after Jesus' birth, the Bible records Herod dying.

Although the Bible does not give us the exact year, there is other historical evidence regarding the year of Herod's death. Some interpret that evidence to mean he died in 4 B.C., which would then put the year of Jesus' birth at 5 B.C. More recently, many have interpreted that evidence to mean that Herod died in 1 B.C., which could put the year of Christ's birth just prior to that, in 2, or 1, B.C.[8] We will now examine special occurrences that took place in the stars and planets, but before we do, let's see what the Bible says about them.

He determines the number of the stars;

he gives all of them their names.

(PSALM 147:4, ESV)

Lift up your eyes on high and see: who created these?

He who brings out their host by number,

calling them all by name, by the greatness of his might,

and because he is strong in power, not one is missing.

(ISAIAH 40:26, ESV)

Although Christians do not worship stars, but God alone, it is awe inspiring to consider God's creative efforts expanding into our galaxy. In fact, in the book of Job, one of the oldest books of the Bible, names of constellations are already mentioned as being placed in the galaxy by God.

...who alone stretched out the heavens

and trampled the waves of the sea;

who made the Bear and Orion,

the Pleiades and the chambers of the south;

who does great things beyond searching out,

and marvelous things beyond number.

(JOB 9:8-10, ESV)

Some have a hard time believing that God placed the stars in the sky and knows them by name. Perhaps seeing the evidence on display through the rest of the book will convince you to believe, as I do, that this indeed is true. As we move into astronomy, I would humbly like to give credit to the Star of Bethlehem video and their website, which led me to this evidence, which I then confirmed through further research.[9] As I followed up on what I learned through additional research, I was encouraged that the claims of that video have been confirmed.

To begin, there is some history you may recollect from school that helps make sense of all of this. You may remember from science class the name Johannes Kepler (December 27, 1571– November 15, 1630). The field of astronomy is indebted to him for a very profound discovery, one that became known as the laws of planetary motion. What I find interesting is that many early astronomers, as was the case with Kepler, were Christians who wanted to learn more about the astronomical events mentioned in Scripture. What Kepler discovered regarding planetary motion is that stars and planets are precise in their continued movements. This has since been confirmed to be true. That is why such planetary movements are known as laws and not theories. We are all actually personally familiar with this today, perhaps without knowing it. You may remember in elementary school going outside on a particular day to witness (but not directly look at) an eclipse that might have been taking place. You may have even recently heard on the news reporters sharing when the next eclipse or extraordinary sun or planetary alignment would take place. This is because we know exactly when these events will take place, like clockwork, due to the laws of planetary motion. What is truly remarkable is what we are now able to do with technology. Because star and planetary movements are precise, we can now not only know their future, but also go back to any minute in history and know with certainty the exact location of stars. How cool is that? That leads us to a very interesting question. What took place in our galaxy, around 2 B.C./1 BC, that could very likely convince us of the year of our Lord?

There is a traditional view of Christmas that I will now need to correct in order to consider the evidence to come. All of us have seen Christmas cards of wise men at the manger of Christ, as though they arrived at that site on the day of His birth. Although it is true that they followed a star, and it is true that they came and gave gifts to Jesus, it was not on the day (or night) of His birth. Here is what the Bible says about the magi's (wise men) visit.

Now <u>after</u> Jesus was born in Bethlehem of Judea in the days of

Herod the king, behold, wise men from the east

came to Jerusalem, saying,

"Where is he who has been born king of the Jews?

For we saw his star when it rose

and have come to worship him."

(MATTHEW 2:1, 2)

And behold, the star that they had seen when it rose

went before them until it came to rest over the place

where the child was. When they saw the star,

they rejoiced exceedingly with great joy.

And <u>going into the house</u> they saw the child

with Mary his mother, and they fell down

and worshiped him.

> **Then, opening their treasures, they offered him gifts,**
>
> **gold and frankincense and myrrh.**
>
> (MATTHEW 2:9-11, ESV)

You may recall that Jesus was born in a stable and then placed in a manger because there was no room in a nearby inn. Here we can clearly see the wise men came to Jesus, *after* He was born, when He was now staying in a house with His parents Mary and Joseph; they were no longer in a stable as on the day of his birth.

Although in regard to the overall story this has little significance, it can impact the accurate dating of Jesus' birth. These wise men were said to begin their quest to Bethlehem because of a star that, to them, indicated the birth of a king. What made this star unique that they would notice it, and what was it about the star that indicated to them a king? Now, it is entirely possible that God could just make a star appear because he wanted to. However, it is interesting to ask the following question. What is the greater miracle? To miraculously make stars appear outside of their planned motions, or to have stars preplanned like clockwork to align just at the right time and place to announce the birth of God's Son and, even more so, His death?

To begin this first revelation, it is important to note that Venus and Jupiter are the two brightest planets (which look like stars) in the sky. What is interesting is that on very rare occasions these planets, as they move in motion, can converge quite closely from our viewing point on earth. This is exactly what happened and in this case their proximity to one another was both brilliant and extraordinary.

So just how close did these planets come from our viewing point on earth? In astronomy, the sky is broken up into a 360-degree "clock" in order to yield a precise way of establishing star positions and movements. To understand this clock, imagine an old-fashioned clock that has a small dash around the edge, one dash for each minute. Now imagine how small 360 dashes would be around that outer edge.

In astronomy, each of the 360 degrees, which are already very small to see, are then broken up into another 60 minutes each. That would be 21,600 dashes! But to go further, each minute is broken into 60 seconds. Our astronomical clock now has 1,296,000 precise measurements. When we talk seconds, from our viewing point on earth, we are talking extremely close increments, especially to the naked eye of these wise men. Equipped with this knowledge, we can now look at what very well may have been the star of Bethlehem. On June 17, 2 B.C., Jupiter and Venus, already the two brightest objects in the galaxy, came together so closely that they appeared from earth to be *one* magnificently brilliant-looking "star." In fact, in this very rare occurrence, they were only six seconds apart! Today it makes the news when Venus and Jupiter come minutes apart. This convergence, in 2 B.C., was one of the closest convergences of these planets in history. It is considered by modern scientists to have been a remarkable event for the people of that day.[10, 11, 12]

There are a couple of other factors to keep in mind regarding the stars in the sky and the people of that day, in particular these magi, or wise men. Not only are these men considered by historians to be scholarly, but people of that day in general are widely held to be more fascinated by star gazing than the general population is today. It was a different time. Due to a lack of media like television and movies, a lack of air pollution, and a hot climate, which prompted people to their rooftops for fresh air, many nights were spent taking in the stars. So when something this rare occurred, people noticed. What we do know is that this was a very special event, and there is a high probability that this juncture of Venus and Jupiter had a role in the wise men's search for King Jesus.

Why, though, did this indicate to them a king was to be born? Those two planets, which appeared to be one massive bright light in the sky, appeared in the constellation Leo. Leo, which is the constellation of a lion, has royal, familial, and kingly attributes. The lion is the symbol of the tribe of Judah, which is the tribe of David, and the family line of Jesus. In addition, the Bible refers to Jesus as the Lion from the tribe of Judah (Revelation 5:5). That is why their convergence, in that constellation, could have indicated to these wise men that a royal one, or king, was to be born. When one begins to research astronomical events that took place around this time, they find that although this joining of the planets is most remarkable, there are other unique astronomical events that took place right around the same time; these, additionally, could have influenced the magi in seeking and finding Jesus. In short, it seems like the stars were dancing in the sky with much splendor at this special time in history.

Due to all of this, I believe the birth of Christ occurred around the turn of 2 to 1 B.C. We will now move from astronomy to the actual prophecies recorded in the Bible about Jesus' birth—and see how they all come together.

Discussion Questions
···

You may want to discuss chapters 10 and 11 together.

1) What is one of your memories as a child, or adult, of an astronomical event? Do you remember what you were told when it would take place? What does this tell us about the movement of planets and stars?

2) Describe what happened with the planets Venus and Jupiter in 1 B.C., and why that convergence could have been part of what the wise men witnessed?

3) Where did the wise men encounter Jesus?

Eleven

The Prophetic Fulfillment of His Birth

Have you ever read the genealogy, or family tree, of Jesus in the King James Version (KJV) of the Bible? The King James Version of Matthew 1 reads as follows.

The book of the generation of Jesus Christ,

the son of David, the son of Abraham.

Abraham begat Isaac; and Isaac begat Jacob; and Jacob begat

Judas and his brethren; And Judas begat Phares and Zara of

Thamar; and Phares begat Esrom; and Esrom begat Aram; And

Aram begat Aminadab; and Aminadab begat Naasson; and

Naasson begat Salmon; And Salmon begat Booz of Rachab;

and Booz begat Obed of Ruth; and Obed begat Jesse;

And Jesse begat David the king.

(MATTHEW 1:1-6a, KJV)

Now, many people, by the fourth or fifth "begat," are about to be gone! *Begat*, by the way, means fathered. So, if this is so boring to read, why did Matthew and Luke both start off their narrative of Jesus' birth, life, death, and resurrection in this manner? It's because it does matter—a lot! We miss this primarily because we are not first-century Jews attempting to follow the Law of Moses and the prophetic message of the Old Testament, but the people of that day were. When they would read the opening of Matthew's account above, they would know the significant purpose that Matthew would be conveying. If we continued reading from Matthew 1:6, where I stopped just above, we would discover the full family line of Jesus. This is important because of what we already learned regarding the Dead Sea Scrolls. Jesus was prophesied to be born from the family line of David. If you keep reading in Matthew, you find that the author indeed traces Jesus' lineage all the way to David, fulfilling the prophecy below—and many others.

Of the increase of his government and of peace
there will be no end, on the throne of David and over his kingdom,
to establish it and to uphold it with justice and with righteousness
from this time forth and forevermore.
The zeal of the LORD of hosts will do this.

(ISAIAH 9:7, ESV)

In addition to God fulfilling this prophecy, you may remember, it was foretold that this Messiah would be born of a virgin. Let's read about how Jesus' conception took place.

In the sixth month the angel Gabriel was sent from God
to a city of Galilee named Nazareth, to a virgin betrothed
to a man whose name was Joseph, of the house of David.
And the virgin's name was Mary. And he came to her and said,
"Greetings, O favored one, the Lord is with you!" But she was

greatly troubled at the saying, and tried to discern
what sort of greeting this might be.
And the angel said to her, "Do not be afraid, Mary,
for you have found favor with God. And behold,
you will conceive in your womb and bear a son,
and you shall call his name Jesus. He will be great and will be
called the Son of the Most High. And the Lord God will give to him
the throne of his father David, and he will reign over the house of
Jacob forever, and of his kingdom there will be no end."
And Mary said to the angel,
"How will this be, since I am a virgin?"
And the angel answered her, "The Holy Spirit will come upon you,
and the power of the Most High will overshadow you;
therefore the child to be born will be called holy—
the Son of God. And behold, your relative Elizabeth in her old age
has also conceived a son, and this is the sixth month with her
who was called barren. For nothing will be impossible
with God." And Mary said, "Behold, I am the servant of the Lord;
let it be to me according to your word."
And the angel departed from her.

(LUKE 1:26-38, ESV)

What a beautiful story. The angel summarizes well what we are
now seeing displayed, both through fulfilled prophecies and in the
stars in the sky: "For nothing will be impossible with God."

Although it is awesome to see God do the impossible, it can
be difficult to accept a miracle when heard through a third party.
This helps us put into context the awkward position that Mary's
fiancé, Joseph, is now faced with. Imagine what Joseph may have
thought after Mary told him she was pregnant! He knows, clearly,

whether he was promiscuous with Mary or not. Since he knows he wasn't, he likely thought Mary must have been with another man. When Mary tells Joseph she is pregnant, through what must have seemed like an impossible-to-believe story from an angel, he is deeply troubled, and considers breaking off their engagement quietly. If people have a hard time believing the virgin conception, they can understand why Joseph would too. Here is what happens next.

Now the birth of Jesus Christ took place in this way. When his mother Mary had been betrothed to Joseph, before they came together she was found to be with child from the Holy Spirit. And her husband Joseph, being a just man and unwilling to put her to shame, resolved to divorce her quietly. But as he considered these things, behold, an angel of the Lord appeared to him in a dream, saying, "Joseph, son of David, do not fear to take Mary as your wife, for that which is conceived in her is from the Holy Spirit. She will bear a son, and you shall call his name Jesus, for he will save his people from their sins." All this took place to fulfill what the Lord had spoken by the prophet:

"Behold, the virgin shall conceive and bear a son, and they shall call his name Immanuel" (which means, God with us). When Joseph woke from sleep, he did as the angel of the Lord commanded him: he took his wife, but knew her not until she had given birth to a son. And he called his name Jesus.

(MATTHEW 1:18-25, ESV)

So far we have heard from the accounts of Matthew and Luke about the story of Joseph, Mary, and the baby Jesus. All have confirmed that Mary was a virgin, just like the prophets foretold. It is interesting to note that this Matthew was one of the twelve apostles of Jesus. Not only did Matthew leave everything to follow Jesus, including his lucrative career as a tax collector, it is strongly believed that after the death of Jesus, Matthew was martyred for his faith in Him. Matthew wrote down the story of Jesus' birth, life, death, and resurrection. One can either believe he was lying or believe that he was telling the truth. We have no record of Matthew ever denying anything he wrote, but we do have a record of him *dying* for what he wrote. If he was lying, why would he die for a lie? Yes, I believe we can trust that God did perform a miracle in the virgin birth, just as He foretold through Scripture.

There is another problem we must address and allow the Bible to solve, if it can. As has already been told, this Messiah is supposed to have been born in Bethlehem, David's hometown. Fulfilling the prophesy of Bethlehem being the birth city of Jesus was not going to be an easy feat. Joseph and Mary are living more than 80 miles from Bethlehem in a town called Nazareth. So how is God going to see that all this comes true?

In those days a decree went out from Caesar Augustus that all the world should be registered. This was the first registration when Quirinius was governor of Syria. And all went to be registered, each to his own town. And Joseph also went up from Galilee, from the town of Nazareth, to Judea, to the city of David, which is called Bethlehem, because he was of the house and lineage of David, to be registered with Mary, his betrothed, who was with child. And while they were there, the time came for her to give birth. And she gave birth to her firstborn son and wrapped him in swaddling cloths and laid him in a manger, because there was no place for them in the inn.

(LUKE 2:1-7, ESV)

God's going to get done what He wants done. God orchestrates a census to be taken, and each person has to go to his hometown, his place of birth, to be registered. Joseph, being from the family line of David, needed, then, to travel to Bethlehem, his family's hometown. I love how this is spoken of. "And while they were there, the time came for her to give birth." Today, doctors can induce the birth of a child through medicine. Before that medicine existed, God, through his power, had his own medicine. Mary did not deliver before she arrived in Bethlehem nor after she and Joseph left Bethlehem. She delivered *in* Bethlehem, just as had been foretold 750 years earlier through the prophet Micah.

But you, O Bethlehem Ephrathah,

who are too little to be among the clans of Judah,

from you shall come forth for me one who is to be ruler in Israel,

whose coming forth is from of old,

from ancient days.

Therefore he shall give them up until the time

when she who is in labor has given birth.

(MICAH 5:2, 3a, ESV)

For the past few chapters we have seen many prophecies fulfilled in the birth of Christ. In addition, we have seen that even the star that is reported in the Bible can be explained by a rare, magnificent conjunction of the planets Venus and Jupiter in the constellation of Leo the lion. It was foretold that a baby would be born a King, from a virgin, from the family line of David, and that the King would come from Bethlehem. It all happened just as God foretold. On top of all of this, Matthew, who reported these things, was martyred for his personal belief in these matters. As we recall, this evidence can provide great fuel to our faith. There is much more wood to put on the fire. We will now turn to the ministry and mission of Jesus Christ.

Discussion Questions

1) Does anyone have an interesting story about the unpre-dictability of going into labor?

2) How did God work to get Jesus born in Bethlehem, and why did He do so?

3) What was the significance of the *begats* at the beginning of Matthew?

4) What prophecy of Christ's birth is most meaningful to you, and why?

Chapter Twelve

Introducing the Lamb of God

Before we move on to the life of Christ and His mission to the cross, it would be worthy of our time to take a prayerful pause to savor how incredible it is that Christ came to earth. To comprehend this in its fullness, we need to step out of the scene and rise above it, so to speak, to gain a panoramic view of what God is doing. From that viewpoint, where we can see both the garden and the babe from Bethlehem, God's story is loosed before us. When God formed Adam and Eve in the garden, we learned that God was "with them" in that garden. God literally spoke with Adam there. This reveals God's desire to be known and have relationship with man. The garden was a wonderful place, and it included the tree of life and the tree of the knowledge of good and evil, which was positioned in the middle. The Bible also describes to us that Heaven is a special and glorious place, and it also has a tree of life (Revelation 22:2). The garden, where we began, and Heaven, where Christians are headed, are types of one another. They both share another very important characteristic. In the garden, and in Heaven, sin was/is not permitted. In the garden, Adam and Eve were given the mission of God to multiply His image and likeness. Unfortunately, after receiving this mission, Adam and Eve sinned, and as a result were removed from the garden and the close presence of God. Ever since this time man has struggled to live for God.

Our sin problem, combined with our distance from God, due to sin, hinders our ability to live for Him. God later gave man a temporary solution to help His people remember Him and live for Him. This solution was for God to come near, displaying His presence in the Most Holy Place of the tabernacle. God had the people literally camp all around the tabernacle to keep Him in view. Although God came nearer to them through this tabernacle, the separation that existed since the garden was still there, and it was on display through the massive, thick curtain that separated the people from God's direct presence. During that season of time in the desert, God not only revealed Himself through the tabernacle, but for the first time He also revealed Himself through the written Word. God delivered to Moses the Torah, the first five books of the Old Testament. Later God's people received the additional writings of the prophets. Through all of this revelation, people could now know much more about who God was and what He desired of them. Despite all of this, it *still* was not the same as it was with Adam and Eve in the beginning. People had never seen God and did not have a direct example of Him to observe and imitate. What I am about to share next is something that is so rare, so very awesome, and so incredibly special to the Christian faith.

Seven hundred years before Jesus' coming, as we have seen, Isaiah prophesied that a son would be born of a virgin and that He would be called Immanuel. We need to bask in the glory of what this means. Two thousand years ago something incredible happened that makes Christianity stand alone. Two thousand years ago the world received Immanuel: *God with us.* Yes, God literally came to be with us. Jesus is God with us. When man struggled to know God and follow Him and to know more about His heart and what He desired, God literally showed up to be with us through the deity of His Son. Here is what is said about Jesus.

Long ago, at many times and in many ways, God spoke to our fathers by the prophets, but in these last days he has spoken to us by his Son, whom he appointed the heir of all things, through whom also he created the world. He is the radiance of the glory of God and the exact imprint of his nature.

(HEBREWS 1:1-3a, ESV)

Incredible. God, who asked us to multiply His image and likeness, came to earth so that we could observe what He is like. Through Jesus we can now observe what God is like. God wanted us to succeed so much in multiplying His image and likeness that He *showed up*. We stand, or rather kneel, in awe, that in Christianity we have Immanuel, God with us, through Jesus. There is no comparison with this in any other religion.

Some may think that although Jesus came, He did not come to earth during my life time. For some, venturing back two thousand years in history can be difficult to grasp. Perhaps what I share next will help. Have you ever watched the NBC *Today Show* segment that celebrates those who turn a hundred years old? During that part of the show we get to see the smiling faces of those who have had the blessing of celebrating their one hundredth birthday and beyond. Sometimes we even get to hear of some of the activities these privileged folks are still enjoying. I marvel at what full lives these people have been able to experience, and the thought of them brings a smile to my face. This illustrates an interesting point. In every generation there are people who are privileged to live more than one hundred years. Do you know what that means? If we go back across the span of just twenty of these lives, we would be with people who may have been a shepherd at the manger of

Christ, or one of the women tending to Jesus at the cross. It's not as long ago as one thinks.

In addition, we are now privileged to have something in our possession of immeasurable value. Earlier in my life, I spent eleven years in the real estate business. At times in that business, people would attempt to make a verbal offer. Our reply as Realtors was always that it needed to be in writing. When one puts it in writing, it becomes legit. We now have the story and message of God, when He was with us in the flesh, in writing! This written Word helps us know so much more about who God is, what He is like, and what He most desires. This written Word, recorded by the apostles, and carried along by the Holy Spirit of God, gives us words and guidance about Jesus Christ, Immanuel, God with us.

We have marveled at His coming. Let's now observe His life beginning with the grand introduction of His ministry.

Just months before Jesus was born of His mother Mary, Mary's relative, Elizabeth, who was still barren in her old age, miraculously was able to conceive and also give birth to a son, who was named John. This John, known as John the Baptist, was prophesied about in the Old Testament as well, as one who was to come and prepare the way for Jesus' ministry. Let's read about what was said about this John the Baptist hundreds of years prior to his birth.

Behold, I will send my messenger,

and he will prepare the way before me.

(MALACHI 3:1a, ESV)

A voice cries: In the wilderness prepare the way of the Lord;

make straight in the desert a highway for our God.

(ISAIAH 40:3, ESV)

John's ministry began just prior to the ministry of Jesus, and he

did indeed prepare the way for God's Son. John the Baptist ministered in the Judean desert wilderness. There, people were attracted to his bold messages, which called on them to repent, be baptized, and turn back to God. That message is for us today. With his
ministry becoming famous, and the crowds gathering around him,
some people were led to ask John if *he* was the Christ. This is how
he responded.

And this is the testimony of John, when the Jews sent priests and
Levites from Jerusalem to ask him, "Who are you?" He confessed,
and did not deny, but confessed, "I am not the Christ." And they
asked him, "What then? Are you Elijah?" He said, "I am not." "Are
you the Prophet?" And he answered, "No." So they said to him,
"Who are you? We need to give an answer to
those who sent us. What do you say about yourself?"
He said, "I am the voice of one crying out in the wilderness,
'Make straight the way of the Lord,' as the prophet Isaiah said."

(Now they had been sent from the Pharisees.) They asked him,
"Then why are you baptizing, if you are neither the Christ,
nor Elijah, nor the Prophet?" John answered them,
"I baptize with water, but among you stands one you do not know,
even he who comes after me, the strap of whose sandal
I am not worthy to untie." These things took place in Bethany
across the Jordan, where John was baptizing.

(JOHN 1: 19-28, ESV)

One can see that the people were indeed looking for the Christ
to come, and they were wondering if John was Him. We see that
John plainly claims to be the one who was to come *before*, in order
to prepare the way for, the Christ. Let's re-enter the story, in the
very next verse, to take in what happens next with John the Baptist.

The next day he saw Jesus coming toward him, and said,
<u>"Behold, the Lamb of God, who takes away the sin of the world!</u>
This is he of whom I said, 'After me comes a man who ranks before
me, because he was before me.' I myself did not know him,
but for this purpose I came baptizing with water,
that he might be revealed to Israel." And John bore witness:
"I saw the Spirit descend from heaven like a dove, and it remained
on him. I myself did not know him, but he who sent me to baptize
with water said to me, 'He on whom you see the Spirit descend
and remain, this is he who baptizes with the Holy Spirit.' And I have
seen and have borne witness that this is the Son of God."

(JOHN 1:29-34, ESV)

When John sees Jesus coming, it is revealed to him that Jesus
is the Messiah. What happens next is a very special moment in
history because John introduces the ministry of Jesus with beautiful imagery that only a student of the Word of God would pick
up. Perhaps, at this point in this book, you are that student. When
John the Baptist saw Jesus coming, he announced the main mission of this Immanuel. "Behold, the lamb of God, who takes away
the sin of the world!" When we see this in its fullness, in our next
chapter, the revelation will overwhelm. John, in this setting, now
has the incredible honor of baptizing Jesus. After He comes up out
of that water, Jesus' ministry begins! Similarly, our true ministry
and destiny also begin when we embrace Jesus for who He is and
what He has done. If we were to read on, we would discover that
John the Baptist had disciples and that he now told them to follow
Jesus instead of himself. He indeed helped pave the way for Jesus'
ministry, as the prophets foretold.

* * * * *

So far we have seen that both Old Testament Scriptures and

John the Baptist declared who Jesus is. But who did *Jesus* say He is? What we will witness next is a dramatic account of when Jesus reveals Himself to the people, and not just any people, but to the people in His very own hometown. It has been argued, rightfully, that there may not be a harder group of people to lead than the people in your own hometown. We have no record of Jesus doing anything unworthy of following, but the Scriptures do say,

**And he said, "Truly, I say to you, no prophet is
acceptable in his hometown."**

(LUKE 4:24, ESV)

It is one thing to minister in your hometown, but this is so much more. Jesus is about to tell them that He is Immanuel! What an incredibly weighty thing to have to reveal of Himself, especially prior to the miracles He would later do to confirm it.

When Jesus reveals Himself, He does it smack dab in the middle of a Jewish synagogue. The daily reading assigned for that day miraculously happens to be from an Old Testament passage that is talking about Jesus. Of course it is. God is remarkable. On top of it all, Jesus happens to be the synagogue reader that day. We did not previously look at this specific passage, but we did look at many others from the same book of Isaiah. When you take in the story we are about to read, I encourage you to put yourself in the room with Jesus. Take your seat in the synagogue. Imagine Him standing up from among the crowd, all the eyes taking notice, and watching and even hearing Him unroll the scroll slowly and carefully. Now picture everyone in the room being extremely quiet, waiting to hear what will be spoken. Imagine every eye steadfastly fixed on Jesus.

**And he came to Nazareth, where he had been brought up.
And as was his custom, he went to the synagogue on the Sabbath
day, and he stood up to read. And the scroll of the**

prophet Isaiah was given to him. He unrolled the scroll
and found the place where it was written,

"The Spirit of the Lord is upon me,

because he has anointed me

to proclaim good news to the poor.

He has sent me to proclaim liberty to the captives

and recovering of sight to the blind,

to set at liberty those who are oppressed,

to proclaim the year of the Lord's favor."

And he rolled up the scroll and gave it back to the
attendant and sat down. And the eyes of all in the
synagogue were fixed on him. And he began to say to them,
"Today this Scripture has been fulfilled in your hearing."

(LUKE 4:16-21, ESV)

Boom! The one you have been waiting for all these years, the one who has long been prophesied to come in your scrolls, *today*, that Scripture has been fulfilled, *in me*. I am the Messiah! This is what Jesus is saying. Love it! Radical! What do you think happens next? Jesus had not yet done much to reveal to these people evidence that would confirm to them that He was who He just said He was. That day, those people ran Him out of town! Remember, the Bible states that no prophet is accepted in his hometown. Even Jesus' own family did not accept this, at least at first. As we will see, in the end they became convinced He was who He said He was. Jesus is still either accepted or rejected by people today. We all have a choice to welcome Him in, or, we can communicate to Him—perhaps not by words, but through our actions—that we would rather He leave town.

One other brief point that may minister to some is that Jesus can identify with rejection. We all face rejection—of many kinds.

It may be because of our status, faith, personality, appearance, or race. Rejection hurts. It is comforting to know that Jesus can identify with the rejection we face. Despite His sacrificial life and miracles, He was rejected often, and ultimately rejected at the cross. Yet despite this He continued to live for God and follow the plan for His life. Don't let rejection keep you from your calling. And know that Jesus has compassion and understanding in the rejection you face. He has offered acceptance, and He desires that we embrace the love and forgiveness He offers.

* * * * *

Over the next three years Jesus poured His life into twelve men who witnessed and even participated with Him in performing miracles. It was important to Him that these men were convinced that He was who He said He was, so that when He departed they would carry on His mission to let the whole world know about Him. He turned water into wine, made the blind see and the lame walk, calmed a storm, walked on water, healed a multitude of sick people, fed thousands of people with almost nothing (twice), and even raised a man from the tomb who had been dead for four days. Ultimately, He beat death time and time again and proved it by showing Himself alive after His own death! The Bible tells us that the crowds thronged around Him wherever He went. Literally, if He would sail across a huge lake, they would race to the other side. If He did not do the miraculous, why would the people have followed Him? They followed Him because they never saw anyone do what He could do.

Throughout the three years of His ministry, Jesus taught many wonderful lessons through stories. Jesus was an incredible storyteller. My heart pleads with whoever is reading this book to have the Bible be the very next book they read. It is the number one–selling book of all time for a reason. It is the most powerful book in the world. In it, God is revealed to us. I am who I am today because of God and how He used both His Spirit and His book to change my life. My heart is saddened by so many who don't know and read the Word of God and are missing out on the incredible guidance and peace God's Word could provide in their lives. Have you heard the expression, regarding weight loss, that diets don't work; rather, one needs to change their lifestyle? Please do not go on a diet; rather, make a lifetime, lifestyle decision to regularly, daily, study and soak in God's love letter, the Bible. Beginning in the New Testament and reading the Gospels of Matthew, Mark, Luke, and John is an incredible place to start. The book of Acts, which comes after John, then records the things Jesus' followers did for the next thirty years after His death. It is an awesome read and inspires us to join Jesus, and them on His mission.

During the three years of Jesus' ministry, on several occasions, He told His followers that one day He would leave them. They did not like hearing about it, and it seems his followers didn't even know how to respond. No one likes to talk about someone they love leaving. It appears to be in our nature as people to avoid this matter. Yet Jesus is found continually reminding them of this fact. It is remarkable that Jesus' ministry lasted only three years and that He died at about the age of thirty-three. This reveals something significant. Jesus had a mission, and His mission did not include a long life here on earth. His mission included suffering and dying young. No matter how many years we live on this earth, it is not long in the face of eternity. Jesus prepared His disciples for His departure, just as he prepared Himself. Sometimes the very things we don't want to think about are the very things we need to consider. Knowing His life was short, Jesus lived life for a purpose. The more we also realize our lives our short, we gain wisdom that inspires us to live for a higher purpose.

So teach us to number our days

that we may get a heart of wisdom.

(PSALM 90:12, ESV)

The question then becomes: what purpose? This book has illustrated that God has a mission for us to reflect and multiply Him in people.

**Simply said, life is about God,
and God is about people.
Therefore, life is about people
knowing God.**

The purpose of this book is to convince us to altar our lives to live for Him. The spelling of altar—A-L-T-A-R—is no mistake. When we arrive at that place in the story, it will all make sense. So onward to the cross we go.

The next chapter contains the best evidence, this side of Heaven, that God is true, His Word can be trusted, and that His Son is the Lamb of God who takes away the sins of the world. I mentioned earlier that Jesus' family initially had a hard time accepting who He said He was. In the end it all changed. Not only was his mother, Mary, at the cross at His death, but His brothers ended up living their lives to proclaim His message, even to the point of their own deaths. They wrote the books of Jude and James. They went from doubt to sold out.

When we experience what they witnessed, we too are inspired to give our lives to serve the One who first gave His.

Questions for Discussion

1) Think deeply, and describe to each other the incredible uniqueness of the fact that in Christianity we have Immanuel.

2) What are some of the things Hebrews 1:1-3 reveals to us?

3) What are some of the things John the Baptist says to describe Jesus?

4) Jesus' life on earth was short. He knew it would be and therefore prepared the disciples for His departure. How would you describe what Jesus focused on for the three years of His ministry?

5) Knowing His life was short, Jesus lived life for a purpose. The more we also realize our lives are short, we gain wisdom that inspires us to live for a higher purpose. In this chapter the author makes the following statement about life's purpose and then shares the verse that follows the statement. How should embracing these things impact the way a Christian lives his or her life?

**Simply said, life is about God,
and God is about people.
Therefore, life is about people
knowing God.**

**So teach us to number our days
that we may get a heart of wisdom.**

(PSALM 90:12, ESV)

Chapter Thirteen

The Lamb of God on a Cross

Toward the end of Jesus' three years of ministry, He performed one of the most profound of His many miracles. He raised a man from the dead. This man, Lazarus, literally came out of his cave-tomb with the grave cloths still wrapped around him since he had been dead four days. Immediately after He performed this miracle, this is what was said.

Many of the Jews therefore, who had come with Mary and had seen what he did, believed in him, but some of them went to the Pharisees and told them what Jesus had done. So the chief priest and the Pharisees gathered the council and said, "What are we to do? For this man performs many signs. If we let him go on like this everyone will believe in him, and the Romans will come and take away both our place and our nation."

(JOHN 11:45-48, ESV)

In order to put this in context, we must understand that Jesus was a Jew with an Israelite lineage. He was following the same faith of God's people throughout the Old Testament that we have been following throughout this book. The difference is that Jesus was now fulfilling what was said about the One who was to come, and in His coming He was now ushering in a new age. Through Jesus, the New Covenant was now going to be superimposed over the Old Covenant. This fulfillment of what the Old Covenant promised was going to bring in sweeping changes to what it would mean to follow God. Change is hard. The Pharisees, the Jews who were in religious authority, were threatened by these changes and Jesus' increasing prominence. Jesus had many run-ins with these Pharisees, because their zeal in their faith was many times misplaced. They added to what the Scriptures taught and seemed to be more concerned with following rules than following God from the heart. They cared more about following the rules of the Sabbath than ministering to people who had needs. With all of the miracles Jesus was performing, and the attention He was receiving, combined with the challenges He made to the Pharisees' religiosity, the Pharisees wanted to have Him killed. As we saw in the passage above, their feeling was that if they could stamp him out, then their position and religion would remain intact. Their strategy could have worked. Except for the fact that Jesus would rise again! In 2012 the Pew Research Center reported that 31.5 percent of the world identifies with Christianity, and only .2 percent of the world identifies with Judaism.[13] They tried to snub out Jesus and, in doing so, Jesus radically changed the world. Christianity is the number one faith group on earth. As we will see, the evidence justifies why this would be so.

Although the Jewish Pharisees were in the religious authority, they were not the governmental authority of the day. The Roman Empire was strong and expansive at this time, and the Romans governed the Jewish people. The Romans were much more secular, and had many gods, but they respected (allowed for) the religion of the people in this region, which at the time was largely Jewish.

With this backdrop, we will now follow the life of Jesus in what is known as His Passion Week, the last week of His life. In our calendar, Passion Week took place the week leading to Easter Sunday. In the Jewish calendar, this is called the month of Nissan (also known as Abib), which is considered the first month of the Jewish year. The month of Nissan commemorates the first month of the Jewish nation, when it received its freedom from the Egyptian pharaoh on the very first Passover. At dusk, on the fourteenth day of Nissan, the Jewish people celebrate Passover, their most significant holiday, in which they remember God's faithfulness on the very first Passover. In that first Passover, God's people were saved from the Destroyer that came over Egypt because they followed God's instructions by sacrificing an unblemished lamb. On the eve of that fourteenth day, the Israelites put the blood of lambs over their doorposts, indicating that they were the people of God. That night, when God saw the blood over their doorposts, they were saved. All firstborn in Egypt died that night, including Pharaoh's own son. In the Israelites' celebration, they would not only recall the night of the Passover, but also how God helped them escape from the Egyptian army through the parting of the sea. After this first Passover, God told them to commemorate this event forever by celebrating the memory of it each year, on this one special day, beginning on the fourteenth day of Nissan. Celebrating Passover is a way for the Jewish people to worship God, remember all He has done, and pass on faith to their children.

In Jesus' day this celebration impacted the whole region and especially the city of Jerusalem. Throngs of people, thousands upon thousands, came to Jerusalem on this particular week to prepare and celebrate. Stone ovens would be preconfigured along the path as one would close in on Jerusalem; the ovens were used for the roasting of the thousands of lambs that would be cooked and eaten on Passover eve. This was a happening! Jerusalem was the place to be. The Temple Mount, a massive permanent structure, which replaced the tent-like tabernacle we learned about earlier, was the place people where people would meet and discuss matters of faith during the week. There also was a huge courtyard where people could hang out. Inside the courtyard was a permanent structure that contained the Holy Place and Most Holy Place; the two separate chambers were separated by a massive veil. These areas were off limits to the people! If you were sitting on the Mount of Olives today, which is a large hill just outside the temple area, you can still see remnants of the walls of this historic Temple Mount. All of these places are real places. It is very easy to locate pictures of these places online. This, then, is the setting for this special Passion Week. Let's now follow the events of the week and see how they can increase our faith.

Now the Passover of the Jews was at hand, and many went up from
the country to Jerusalem before the Passover to purify themselves.
They were looking for Jesus and saying to one another
as they stood in the temple, "What do you think?
That he will not come to the feast at all?"
Now the chief priests had given orders that if anyone knew where
he was, he should let them know so that they might arrest him.

(JOHN 11:55-57, ESV)

Jerusalem was an extremely dangerous place for Jesus. The religious establishment picked up stones to stone Him to death on multiple times prior to this, but He had escaped (John 8:59; 10:31-39). Jesus' disciples tried to warn Him not to go back to Jerusalem for this reason (John 11:8). If our lives were being threatened, we would likely avoid the place where someone wanted to kill us. Jesus does just the opposite! He boldly, and for the next several days, walks from the little village of Bethany just a couple of miles over the Mount of Olives into Jerusalem and mixes it up with His opponents and disciples right in the temple court.

Just prior to entering Jerusalem, six days before the Passover, on a Saturday, Jesus is given a celebratory meal in Bethany. The meal is being put on by the family of Lazarus (the one Jesus raised from the dead) to honor and thank Jesus for raising him. At that meal, a woman takes perfume and anoints the feet of Jesus with ointment. Some question why such an expensive thing would be put on Jesus' feet. In that day, many times when people died, they were perfumed prior to their burial. Jesus responds to these questions by telling the people at this meal that this woman is preparing Him for His death. He knew His mission was to die.

On Sunday, now four days before Passover, Jesus rides into town as something like a rock star of today, on a donkey, just as was prophesied (Zechariah 9:9). This event has become known as the Triumphal Entry into Jerusalem.

Most of the crowd spread their cloaks on the road, and others cut branches from the trees and spread them on the road. And the crowds that went before him and followed him were shouting, "Hosanna to the Son of David! Blessed is he who comes in the name of the Lord! Hosanna in the Highest!"

(MATTHEW 21:8, 9, ESV)

Hosanna means: *Save us.* Also notice the reference to the One who was coming from the family line of David. This attention He received would only further the Pharisees' desire to have Him killed. The words the people were shouting were actually from an Old Testament prophecy about the coming Messiah, from Psalm 118. Jesus did not enter Jerusalem, in other words, unnoticed. This stirred the Pharisees up all the more. You may remember, this is the Sunday known as Palm Sunday, which comes a week prior to Easter. Many times churchgoers are given a palm branch to remember this bold day of Jesus' arrival in Jerusalem. For the next several days, then, Jesus mixes it up with both His disciples and opponents in the temple courts.

As we close in on Thursday, final preparations are now being made for the feast of Passover. Passover begins at sunset on that day and continues through sunset on Friday. During the day Thursday, Jesus asks some of His disciples to prepare a place for them to celebrate the Passover together. They don't know it yet, but this will be His last night with them. During the evening, as they recline around a knee-high table, Jesus solemnly gains their attention. Matthew, one of Jesus' twelve apostles, who was in that upper room with Jesus, records for us what is said at this evening ceremony.

Now as they were eating, Jesus took bread, and after blessing it broke it and gave it to the disciples, and said, "Take, eat, this is my body." And he took a cup, and when he had given thanks he gave it to them, saying, "Drink of it, all of you, for this is my <u>blood of the covenant</u>, which is poured out for many for the <u>forgiveness of sins</u>. I tell you I will not drink again of this fruit of the vine until that day I drink it new with you in my Father's Kingdom."

(MATTHEW 26:26-29, ESV)

We now begin to bring to light some of those key Old Testament artifacts and dust them clean to see their full meaning. We learned earlier that in the Old Testament, when God made a covenant with his people, the leadership was to offer a sacrifice and the covenant would be sealed with blood. Also, as we noted prior, six hundred years earlier, Jeremiah told us that:

"Behold, the days are coming, declares the Lord, when I will make a new covenant..."

(JEREMIAH 31:31a, ESV)

"I will forgive their inequity, and I will remember their sin no more."

(JEREMIAH 31:34b, ESV)

Jesus shares with His men that night, on the eve of Passover, in this Last Supper communion experience, that He is ushering in God's New Covenant and that this wine is a symbol of the blood that will be shed to bring in the New Covenant age. Jesus confirmed that His blood would be poured out for many for the forgiveness of sins.

During this meal, sadly, one of Jesus' disciples, Judas, departs to betray Jesus. The disciples did not yet fully understand what is taking place, or how quickly this would all go down. In one moment they are with Jesus, in an upper room enjoying a celebratory meal with Him. In just over twelve hours, He will die for them and for the world. That night, as in a typical Jewish Passover, they sang a hymn together. Interestingly, the typical hymn sung during this special night encompasses Psalms 113-118, the very words that were shouted at the triumphal entry. They then depart the upper room and go to a place they commonly went for prayer, called the Garden of Gethsemane, which is just a short distance across the Kidron Valley from the temple mount area at the base of the Mount of Olives.

In this place of prayer, Jesus, knowing what is about to take place, goes a short distance from the disciples for a heartfelt time of prayer. It is one of the times we see Jesus experience being fully human (as well as God) and the magnitude of emotions that come from the anticipation of the severity of an upcoming crucifixion. Knowing what was about to happen, He sweats what was like drops of blood.

> **And he withdrew from them**
> **[his apostles] about a stone's throw,**
> **and knelt down and prayed, saying,**
> **"Father, if you are willing, remove this cup from me.**
> **Nevertheless, not my will, but yours, be done."**
>
> (LUKE 22:41, 42, ESV)

When Jesus finished praying, Judas, the traitor, came and kissed Jesus to indicate to the band of soldiers, who came to arrest Him, which one was Jesus. In a brief scuffle, Peter cut off one of the ears of the men who came to arrest him with a sword. Jesus tells Peter to put down the sword, and then Jesus heals the man's ear. Jesus is amazing. Jesus is then taken captive for interrogation. The interrogators include the two high priests, Annas and Caiaphas, King Herod, and the Roman governor, Pontius Pilate. The high priests wanted Jesus killed for claiming He had authority from God and that He was God's Son, but they did not have the actual legal authority to put Him to death. So they riled up the people and took Him to Pilate, who would be the ultimate decision maker (on behalf of God) in this matter. During these interrogations with Herod and Pilate, both of these leaders attempted to pull out of Jesus a radical claim about Himself in order to help justify His death. Jesus in both cases during part of the questioning withheld any response. This sparked even more frustration from the interrogators. Jesus did not defend Himself. He did not respond in an effort to save His life, because He knew it was His mission to give His life. This fulfilled what was spoken by the prophet Isaiah seven hundred years earlier.

He was oppressed and afflicted, yet he opened not his mouth;
like a lamb that is led to the slaughter, and like a sheep
that before its shearers is silent, so he opened not his mouth.

(ISAIAH 53:7a, ESV)

How is it possible that Isaiah could predict, so many hundreds of years earlier, what would take place, if it were not for God giving Isaiah those words? Remember, we now know, with the indisputable evidence of the Dead Sea Scrolls, that all of these prophecies predate Jesus.

Jesus is then beaten severely and is made to carry His cross to the place of His martyrdom. Do you remember the story of Isaac carrying the wood for his would-be sacrifice? Do you remember Abraham's words that day?

Abraham said, "God will provide for himself the lamb for a burnt offering, my son."

(GENESIS 22:8a, ESV)

These are amazing examples of God foreshadowing many years earlier what was now taking place. God knew what He was doing, and He had a plan to weave together events that would show us His glory. Do you see? God, in Jesus is providing the offering.

In this pseudo trial, Pilate eventually gives in to the Pharisees and the people the Pharisees were able to muster up to call on Pilate to crucify Jesus. This should not surprise us. Jesus was claiming to be the Son of God, and not everyone saw the miracles. The Pharisees wanted him killed; many in the religious establishment got the people to see Jesus as a self-propagator. After all, claiming to be the Son of God is a weighty claim. Some may have a hard time understanding why, if He had special power from God, Jesus would allow this to happen. If He indeed was who He said He was, this would be, in their minds, His chance to prove it. They did not understand that the most powerful thing He could do was die. And they certainly did not think He would then rise from the dead.

Jesus, now in agony, has to carry His cross up a hill. It was a painful walk, and many shouted at Him along the way. As Jesus carries this cross, two thieves are also preparing to be killed that day with Him. These thieves are an important part of the story. Isaiah said earlier:

And they made his grave with the wicked and with a rich man in his death, although he had done no violence and there was no deceit in his mouth.

(ISAIAH 53:9, ESV)

These thieves, who were being punished for their crimes, fulfill the fact that Jesus would share the grave with the wicked in His death. Skipping ahead briefly, when Jesus finally died, a rich man, Joseph of Arimathea, was granted permission to give Jesus his own tomb as a place of burial. God has again fulfilled His Word by giving Jesus a rich man's burial, just as was foretold.

The hilltop where these men were killed was called Golgotha, which is translated as: "Place of a Skull." If you pull up a picture online you will see why the hill is called Place of a Skull as the hillside has rock formations that look very much like a skull. It is still present today.

Jesus and the thieves are then nailed by their hands and feet to their crosses. Imagine the sound of the large nails being pounded by weighty hammers to the cross. *Clang! Clang!* Even with such brutality, when Jesus is raised up on His cross, He prays to the Father on behalf of the people who nail Him and mock Him.

And Jesus said, "Father, forgive them,
for they know not what they do."
And they cast lots to divide his garments.

(LUKE 23:34, ESV)

What an amazing expression of forgiveness and grace. That is the kind of leadership that compels us to follow. It is also interesting that the soldiers cast lots to divide Jesus' garments. Casting lots is a random way of figuring out a decision or a winner. Kind of like flipping a coin. I am not sure if it was due to impoverished conditions that these clothes were of value, or if it these clothes could have been some type of trophy, but here is what we do know. Psalm 22, a psalm that Jesus quotes from while on the cross, says the following:

For dogs encompass me; a company of evil doers encircles me; they
have pierced my hands and feet—I can count all my bones—

they stare and gloat over me; they divide my garments among them, and for my clothing they cast lots.

(PSALM 22:16-18, ESV)

Nearly a thousand years earlier, this was written and yet it is all coming to pass, just as foretold. Oh, how everyone needs to know all of this information. Are you beginning to believe all the more that God is working all of this out? Jesus, on this cross, is encircled by evildoers who have put Him there, He is pierced in His hands and feet, many are staring at Him, and His garments are divided by casting lots. God wants us to believe and has given us evidence to believe!

While on the cross, at noon on that Friday, darkness came over the land. We are not told how, but only that it occurred.

Now from the sixth hour [noon] there was darkness over all the land until the ninth hour. [3pm]

(MATTHEW 27:45, ESV)

It is amazing, but does not surprise me, that after all we have seen with Jesus' birth, that when God was going to sacrifice His Son, He would line it up with astronomical happenings in the galaxy. The sun being darkened was also prophesied to occur by the prophet Joel five hundred years earlier.

And it will come to pass afterward, that I will pour out my Spirit on all flesh; your sons and your daughters shall prophesy, your old men shall dream dreams, and your young men shall see visions. Even on the male and female servants in those days I will pour out my Spirit. And I will show wonders in the heavens and on the earth, blood and fire and billows of smoke. The sun shall be turned to darkness and the moon to blood before the great and awesome day of the Lord comes.

**And it shall come to pass that everyone
who calls on the name of the Lord shall be saved.**

(JOEL 2:28-32a, ESV)

This is not the last time we will look at this passage. In this instance, we see it was foretold that on a special day many things will occur, one of which is darkness, and as we see here it went dark the day of Jesus' death. What is interesting is that this darkness may also be confirmed by the Olympic Games. The Olympics were a big deal at the time of Jesus and the apostles. Without knowing the exact date, it is recorded that during the 202nd Olympiad, which may have been in the spring of 33 A.D., there was an eclipse of the sun and a reference to an earthquake, which also could have caused the sun to go dark.[14]

Three hours after being nailed to this cross, the strength of these three men is running out, and Jesus knows His time is about to end. Jesus then cries out in His native tongue.

"My God, my God, why have your forsaken me?"

(MATTHEW 27:46b, ESV)

At first glance it seems that Jesus is questioning why God would let Him die, which doesn't make sense if Jesus knew His purpose was to die. In actuality, Jesus was quoting Scripture. Amazingly, Psalm 22 contains many things that came true in the death of Christ. Jesus knowing the Scriptures, and that He came to fulfill them, quotes directly from Psalm 22, which says:

My God, my God, why have you forsaken me?

(PSALM 22:1a, ESV)

Not surprisingly, Jesus was thirsty on the cross, and He told his mother, and others, who were painfully watching Him die, "I thirst." In their proximity, the soldiers had some wine vinegar, a long hyssop branch, and a sponge through which they could reach up to Jesus' mouth. Jesus then received fluid from this branch, which fulfilled yet another historic psalm.

And for my thirst they gave me sour wine to drink.

(PSALM 69:21b, ESV)

The next and very last words powerfully reveal a great deal. From the cross Jesus speaks the words that fulfill what He came to do.

When Jesus had received the sour wine, he said,
"It is finished,"
and he bowed his head and gave up his spirit.

(JOHN 19:30, ESV)

The word used for "finished" in the Scriptures is the Greek word *teleo*. It means to "bring to a close, or to execute, fulfill, or complete a command," or "to pay in such a manner what is necessary to fulfill what is required." Such as paying a debt. In Jesus' last words, He proclaims that He accomplished what was preplanned and set out before him to complete, fulfill, and pay: to die for the sins of the world.

This being a Friday, and with sunset now approaching, it was nearly Saturday. For the Jewish people that is the Sabbath day, a day of rest. Pilate did not want the bodies to remain on the cross for the Sabbath day, so the soldiers decide to take matters into their own hands. What is amazing is that, even in doing so, it is shown they really are being directed by the hands of God.

Jesus is now dead on the cross, but the thieves, without the power to give up their spirits, like Jesus, are still alive. Now if one is in charge of ensuring the death of another, the sooner it occurs, for the sake of time, the better. So in order to ensure this is all over before the Sabbath, the soldiers go to the thieves with a club and brutally smash their legs, breaking them. This gruesome act prevents the thieves from holding themselves up on the cross. With this pain and lack of power, they will now die quickly of asphyxiation. After breaking their legs, the man with the club moves on to Jesus and here is what happens next.

> So the soldiers came and broke the legs of the first,
> and of the other who had been crucified with him.
> But when they came to Jesus and saw
> that he was already dead, they did not break his legs.
> But one of the soldiers pierced his side with a spear
> and at once there came out blood and water.
>
> (JOHN 19:32-34, ESV)

They broke the legs of one thief and then the other, but when they got to Jesus, since He was dead, and they simply wanted to make sure He was good and dead, they pierced His side with a spear and He shed His blood. Why did it all happen this way, and how does this reveal not just the hand of God, but the fulfillment of God in the death of Jesus Christ? It happened this way because God had a plan and part of the plan was to reveal to you and me that we can trust Him. Before revealing this, we will make sure we put it all in context so that our understanding comes from deep within.

In the Old Covenant, a lamb was offered at the tabernacle for the temporary atonement of one's sin. In the New Covenant, Jesus is the once-and-for-all final Lamb of God who takes away the sins of the world. This must be received by faith. So then, how can we know this is true? In short, how can we know Jesus is this final Lamb of God who takes away our sins? What we are about to see is that God intricately follows His own rules to confirm all this for you and me.

Many, reading the New Testament account of Jesus' death on a cross, would read the next verse, words spoken by Jesus on the eve of His death, and simply keep reading without seeing the grand fulfillment that is on display.

**And he said to them, "I have earnestly desired
to eat this Passover with you before I suffer."**

(LUKE 22:15, ESV)

The reason, for most people, that this verse does not catch their eye is because we are not first-century Jews, and many don't know their Old Testament well enough to see what is taking place. By now we all know that the Passover is a hugely special day in the Jewish calendar, one that remembers the glorious day when God saved His people with the sacrifice of a lamb and the blood of the lamb over their doorpost, signifying they believed and followed God's instructions. By doing so, the people were saved and freed that day.

You will remember that the Passover is only one day out of 365 days each year. One day in 365 days is, statistically, .27 percent. That is less than one-third of just a 1 percent chance that something would happen on that day, versus any other of the 365 days on the calendar. In your mind, take a monthly calendar, the kind with the squares on it for each day. Imagine going to April 3, and marking that one square red. Now cut up all the days of the year into squares including that one and put them all in a box. At this point you will have 365 squares in that box. Now blindfold yourself and reach in the box and pick out one square. The odds are very miniscule that you would pick out the red marked square. Yet that is what God did, and as you will soon see, orchestrated as the grand conductor. If Jesus would have died on any other day, we would not have this amazing evidence. It is remarkable, in fact amazing, that Jesus Christ died and shed His blood, and not just on any day, but on that one special day, Passover, indicating that He indeed is God's Passover Lamb.

Besides the fact He died on that day, what other evidence did God make part of this story to prove this to us?

You may remember the requirement, at Passover, that the lamb that is to be used could not just be any lamb, but was to be an unblemished one. The lamb would literally be inspected to ensure it was a worthy sacrifice.

Jesus, too, was unblemished and the Scriptures talk much about this. He was the only person to ever live without sin. He fulfilled God's requirement. He, being sinless, was found worthy to be the ultimate sacrifice.

For our sake he [God] made him [Jesus] to be sin who knew no sin,
so that in him we might become the righteousness of God.

(2 CORINTHIANS 5:21, ESV)

...knowing that you were ransomed
from the futile ways
inherited from your forefathers,
not with perishable things such as silver or gold,
but with the precious blood of Christ,
like that of a lamb without blemish or spot.

(1 PETER 1:18, 19, ESV)

...how much more will the blood of Christ, who through the
eternal Spirit offered himself without blemish to God, purify
our conscience from dead works to serve the living God.
Therefore he is the mediator of a new covenant,
so that those who are called may receive the promised eternal
inheritance, since a death has occurred that redeems them from
the transgressions committed under the first covenant.

(HEBREWS 9:14, 15, ESV)

I marvel at how all of these signs fan our faith into flames as we gain full understanding. In addition to the lamb being unblemished, when sacrificed on the eve of Passover, it was to be sacrificed whole, without its bones broken. Below are the instructions given, nearly two thousand years prior to Christ, on how to rightfully prepare the Passover Lamb.

...and you shall not break any of its bones.

(EXODUS 12:46b, ESV)

When Jesus died on that cross, and they wanted to have the thieves die and all their bodies taken down prior to the Saturday Sabbath, as we have seen, this is what happened.

So the soldiers came and broke the legs of the first, and of the other who had been crucified with him. But when they came to Jesus and saw that he was already dead, they did not break his legs. But one of the soldiers pierced his side with a spear and at once there came out blood and water.

(JOHN 19:32-34, ESV)

Amazing! God is going to make sure that His requirements for the final Lamb are fulfilled. Marvelously, on top of the bones of Jesus not being broken, despite both thieves being broken, neither thief is pierced, but when they get to Jesus and see that He had already died, and now simply wanting to make sure He's dead, they pierce Him in His side, and His blood is shed. So why was Jesus the only one pierced?

Because God keeps His Word! Look what was written seven hundred years earlier.

But he was pierced for our transgressions; he was crushed for our inequities; upon him was the chastisement that brought us peace, and with his wounds we are healed. All we like sheep have gone

astray; we have turned—every one—to his own way;
and the Lord has laid on him the iniquity of us all.

(ISAIAH 53:5, 6, ESV)

For thousands of years God required a sacrifice in order to for-give the sins of man. Despite this method of atonement, man continued to sin. God foretold that one day He would make a New Covenant in which He would remember our sins no more. When God makes a covenant, a sacrifice is required, and blood is used to ratify the covenant. While we, God's people, were still in sin, God chose to make a once-and-forever sacrifice to restore us to Himself and forgive our sins. He did this by taking His one and only Son, Jesus Christ, and sacrificing Him on a cross. God had His Son shed blood to forgive and remove what was in the way of our relationship with Him, our sins.

The next thing that happens when Jesus dies is that in the tem-ple, which is not far away, the curtain that separated the Holy Place from the Most Holy place is torn in two.

And Jesus cried out in a loud voice
and gave up and yielded his spirit.
And behold, the curtain of the
temple was torn in two, from top to bottom.

(MATTHEW 27:50, 51a, ESV)

This was a significant miracle of God that took place right at Jesus' death, and it symbolizes God's desire for us to draw near to Him once again. Jesus' death ushered in a new age, one in which, as Jeremiah prophesied, we would all know God, from the "least to the greatest" (Jeremiah 31:34). The Most Holy Place, which could only be accessed by the high priest, was now open to all. God, through the sacrifice of His Son, opened the way for our fellowship to him through the removal of our sin, which was creating the barrier. The presence of God was going to be able to come nearest to us since the Garden of Eden. The sin of one man, Adam, which broke the bridge of closeness with God, was now rebuilt through the forgiveness granted by the sacrifice of God's man, Jesus.

> **Therefore, as one trespass [Adam's Sin]**
>
> **led to the condemnation for all men,**
>
> **so one act of righteousness [Jesus' Sacrifice]**
>
> **leads to justification and life for all men.**
>
> **For as by the one man's disobedience [Adam]**
>
> **the many were made sinners,**
>
> **so by one man's obedience [Jesus]**
>
> **the many will be made righteous.**
>
> (ROMANS 5:18, 19, ESV)

We have noted that as the garden and Heaven were, and are, places in which sin is not permitted, we now see how it is that man, who has sin, can receive the blessing of Heaven.

Through God's forgiveness we receive righteousness, which is right standing with God. This right standing was not made because we did it all right, but rather because Jesus became the once and final sacrifice who takes away our sin to make us right. Through Jesus' sacrifice, the sin that made us wrong has been forgiven, making us right. In this way we are made right for Heaven. Our sin had to be dealt with. A price needed to be paid for our sin. A sacrifice, as has been displayed, has always been required. This leaves you, me, and everyone in the world with a dramatic choice. To pay for our sin ourselves, in separation from God now and forever, or place our faith in Jesus, the Lamb of God, who was sacrificed to reconcile us back to God.

The opening illustration of this book indicated that mankind is caught in a rip current that separates each individual man and woman from God. It is called sin, and it is sweeping us out to sea. Jesus came to rescue us from the rip current of sin and to restore us to a relationship with Him. Jesus did what was needed to rescue us. He died as the unblemished Lamb of God, the final sacrifice for sin. Our part to play is to believe. To have an inner conviction that this is true. To believe that there is a consequence for sin. That a payment is needed. Once we believe in our desperate need to be rescued (forgiven of our sin), we can then respond by raising our hand and asking to be rescued. We do that through faith in our rescuer, Jesus. When we see it rightly, we discover that the only way to Heaven is through forgiveness of the sin that separates us from entering. We also become convinced that the only way this forgiveness can be offered is by the sacrifice of Jesus. We can no longer bring a lamb to be offered. The final one already has been slain. *When we believe in Jesus as Lord, our sin is nailed to the cross rather than being nailed to us.* In this way we are given grace, forgiveness, and eternal life.

...having been buried with him in baptism, in which you were also raised with him through faith in the powerful working of God, who raised him from the dead. And you, who were dead in your trespasses and the uncircumcision of your flesh, God made alive together with him, forgiven us all our trespasses, by canceling the record of debt that stood against us with its legal demands. This he set aside, <u>nailing it to the cross.</u>

(COLOSSIANS 2:12-14, ESV)

The key to all of this is believing it is true. Jesus is the Lamb of God whose sacrifice can take away the sins of anyone in the world, but it must be personally received by each person through faith. That is why, throughout this book, we have explored evidence that helps us to believe. When we believe, we then receive. So it is very important that we take ownership individually so we can believe. All of the prophetic fulfillments we have seen over the last several chapters give us the confidence to believe.

Bringing these fulfillments together now, for the glory of God... Jesus was born in the family line of David, of a virgin, from the city of Bethlehem, just as was written. There is evidence for the star of the Savior's birth, coming from a joining in the sky of the planets Venus and Jupiter, shining brightly on earth. When Jesus came, He lived a sinless life. Despite all of the strife he faced, he did amazing things, like raising Lazarus to new life. His hands were marked and the sun went dark. He died on that specific day as a Passover lamb, clearly displaying that God had a plan. He shared a grave with wicked thieves, also helping us believe. His bones were not broken, just as was spoken; His side was pierced, it was fierce; He shed his blood, like a lamb would; the veil was torn, the people scorned, His mother mourned, He wore a crown of thorns; and after he died, He was buried in a rich man's tomb, just as Isaiah prophesied.

The grave could not hold Him, soon He would rise, and then more than five hundred people would see him alive. The disciples were martyred, maintaining this was true, confirming this story to me and to you. Faith in Jesus is what we all need. When one believes, forgiveness and eternal life is what they receive.

We started our story at the beginning of this book focusing on some swimmers who were caught in a rip current and desperately tried to swim into the current. Eventually, they came to the realization that they needed a rescuer. They could not save themselves. Nineteen years ago I finally came to the understanding that I was a sinner and that my sin prevented me from a relationship with God and would prevent me from going to Heaven. No matter how hard I tried, I could never be good enough to make it. Heaven is a perfect place, and none of us are perfect. I finally came to realize that I needed a sacrifice for my sin to be forgiven. If we make Jesus the Lord of our lives and our Savior, our sins are then passed over. Why pay for our sin when Jesus was willing to allow it to be placed on Him?

When I received enough knowledge to understand more fully, I raised my hand in faith and said, "Jesus, rescue me." And rescue He did. God desires to rescue all of us from the rip current of sin; the way we do this is to believe in Him. If you never have confessed with your mouth Jesus as Lord, why not pray to him now? Go ahead, bend a knee and say this prayer from your heart, out loud to Jesus. He hears you.

God,
I have come to realize that I am a sinner
and that my sin keeps me from You
now and forever.
I now understand that in
Your great love You sent Your son, Jesus,
to be the final Lamb of God
who takes away the sins of the world.
I believe in Jesus
and I willingly receive Him
as the Lord of my life.
I believe You conquered sin by rising from the dead.
Thank You for sending Him to forgive me.
Please fill me with Your Holy Spirit,
and help me to live a life
that is pleasing to You.
In Jesus' name.

Amen.

Discussion Questions
....

It may be a good idea to spend two weeks on this material. There is something powerful about each person reading in their own Bibles, from the prophecies to the fulfillments. In this way we have greater ability to take ownership of our own faith.

1) The evening of the Last Supper Jesus shares the bread and wine representing His body and blood. In doing so He states to his disciples (Matthew 25) that this was the cup of the New Covenant.

2) What Old Testament prophecy regarding a covenant was Jesus fulfilling? (See Jeremiah 31:31-34.)

3) Why did Jesus use a symbol of blood to usher in this covenant? (See Exodus 24:3-8.)

4) As a reminder, what was the significance of the Dead Sea Scrolls?

5) Read and comment on the Old Testament prophecy and New Testament fulfillment leading to Jesus' death.

    a. Isaiah 53:7 _____ John 19:9

    b. Isaiah 53:9 _____ Luke 23:32-43;
        _____ Matthew 27:57-60

    c. Psalm 22:16-18 _____ Luke 23:34

    d. Joel 2:28-32 _____ Matthew 27:45

    e. Psalm 22:1 _____ Matthew 27:46

    f. Psalm 69:21 _____ John 19:28-30

6) What would most people read, and not really notice, regarding the day of Jesus' death? How does His death on Passover show the hand of God? How were people protected at the first Passover? How are our sins passed over (Romans 3:23-26, ESV), and therefore, how are we saved today?

7) What is the statistical chance of Jesus dying on that *one day* out of the 365 days in each calendar year?

8) What are some of the evidences, on top of the miraculous day of His death, that show Jesus was indeed the Lamb of God who takes away the sins of the world?

> (For more, see below.)
>
> a. Exodus 12:46 _____ John 19:31-34
>
> b. Isaiah 53:5, 6 _____ John 19:31-34
>
> *(Note: In case group members have questions about what is meant by the day of Preparation mentioned in John 19:31, this simply relates to the fact that it was a Friday and the next day was a Saturday, a Sabbath. Friday was considered a day of Preparation so that people could prepare for not working on the Sabbath.)*

9) Imagine if we could figure the complete probability of the statistics in all of this. Example: What are the chances Jesus would die on a Passover; that His bones would not be broken, despite the two thieves' legs being broken; that Jesus' side would be pierced and the two thieves not pierced; the sun darkened at the same time, as prophesied; and much more. It would be astronomical! (More will be added to this later as well.)

10) Is faith in Jesus as the Lamb of God who takes away the sins of the world required for salvation? Why or why not?

11) Did anyone, or would anyone, like to follow the prayer at the end of the chapter in order to make official their trusting in Jesus Christ as their Sacrificial Lamb, Savior, and Lord? (See Romans 10:9.)

Chapter Fourteen

The Cross to Pentecost

After Jesus' death on Passover "Good Friday," the disciples, likely filled with fear, are found hiding out in a home. Their fear is not unwarranted. Their leader was just killed for proclaiming He was God, and it would seem likely that if they promoted His teaching, their lives could be in jeopardy as well. On top of this, they are now without their leader, who has led them courageously for the past three years. To make matters worse, Peter, the most likely candidate to now lead the men, has just denied the Christ three times. In his grief and disappointment in himself, he is not likely up to the task of leading. The disciples, likely in a state of shock, must be very uncertain as to what the future holds. They had given up their lives and careers to follow Jesus, and now they are afraid for their very own lives. We know that these men go on to live amazing, courageous lives for Jesus and His mission to save the world. So then, what changed them? How did they recover and gain the confidence, faith, and strength to continue the selfless mission?

That question is answered by two very important miracles of

God: the resurrection and the Spirit that came at Pentecost. The first gave the apostles confidence and the second gave them spiritual power and conviction to take Jesus' mission to the world. Christianity has since spread all around the globe! Since the resurrection of Jesus, Christianity has become the number one religion in the world. I believe, among other reasons, it is because Christianity has the best evidence and the aid of the Spirit of God. In Christianity, Jesus came back from the dead. If that is true, everything changes. It certainly did for Jesus' disciples. Jesus had a mission for these guys to go and make disciples of all nations. To spread His message and make more followers of Himself. In order to do that effectively, they needed to be convinced that Jesus was who He said He was: God with us. The resurrection not only helped confirm all the miracles Jesus did before that momentous event, it also proved that Jesus was God and had victory over death. Despite Jesus telling them beforehand that they would see Him again, they did not seem to have much hope in His resurrection when they were hiding out on Saturday and Sunday. But I can't blame them. Think about it...who have you seen rise from the dead? Have you ever heard of someone getting hung on a cross, pierced in their side with a spear, and then, after being placed in a tomb, coming back to life again? The resurrection is astonishing. If Jesus really beat death by rising from the dead and showing Himself to His disciples, then He truly must be God! Fortunately, Jesus' resurrection is extremely well attested to. He came back over and over again and showed Himself not only to his disciples but to five hundred people over a period of forty days to affirm, and confirm, that He indeed came back from the dead. The apostles John and Matthew, who were just two of the many eyewitnesses to these resurrection visits, wrote the Gospels that carry their names. I strongly encourage anyone wanting to grow in their faith to read the end of these two books as they recount Jesus' postresurrection visits. I think it is convincing to note that nearly every apostle of Christ has a written record of dying for proclaiming the message of Christ and His resurrection. I think it is safe to say that these apostles are either lying or telling the truth. The thing is, if they were lying, wouldn't they then know that they were lying? Of course. So then, if they were lying, why would they die for a lie? Yet there is no record of any of these disciples denying what they saw, heard, and touched.

They were willing to die because they could not deny what they saw with their own eyes.

I love the way John the Apostle opens his letter known as 1 John.

That which was from the beginning, which we have heard, which we have seen with our eyes, which we looked upon and have touched with our hands, concerning the word of life— the life was made manifest, and we have seen it, and testify to it and proclaim to you the eternal life, which was with the Father and was made manifest to us— that which we have seen and heard we proclaim also to you, so that you too may have fellowship with us; and indeed our fellowship is with the Father and with his Son Jesus Christ. And we are writing these things so that our joy may be complete.

(1 JOHN 1:1-4, ESV)

When I read what John and the others wrote about Jesus and His resurrection, and know that they were willing to die for what they proclaimed, it helps me be convinced. When I add that to the specific prophecies fulfilled concerning Jesus' birth, and especially His death, I am won over to place my faith in and follow Jesus. It also fans into flame my faith recalling that the Dead Sea Scrolls undeniably confirm all the prophecies about Jesus were written *before* Jesus. Jesus dying on that one special day, the Passover, versus any of the other 364 days in a calendar year, inspires me to believe that Jesus is indeed is the Lamb of God who takes away the sins of the world.

I desire so deeply that people get rooted in this knowledge. Increased knowledge of the evidence leads to faith, and faith leads to salvation. One of the reasons this book is loaded with Scripture, and the study questions for small groups are placed at the close of each chapter, is because there is power in taking ownership in this knowledge personally. I hope readers personally and/or in small groups open the Word of God and examine the questions and Scriptures together. The more one personally studies and sees the evidence for themselves, the easier it is to believe. There is a common belief in the world today, by many, that the more one knows the less one believes. The fact is, just the opposite is true. The more one learns and studies the evidence, the easier it is to believe. With all due respect, I believe the reason many don't believe in Christ is because they simply have not taken the time consider the evidence. As the Scriptures say:

You will seek me and find me,
when you seek me with all your heart.

(JEREMIAH 29:13, ESV)

My hope is that this book will be read by believers to both inspire them personally and then to share this book with nonbelievers and seekers so they learn evidence that can lead to faith and their salvation.

We have already seen so many great reasons to believe, but now we will add one more powerful, prophetic fulfillment that may be one of the most astounding evidences of all. To pull this together we are going to move on in our story fifty days from death of Jesus on the Jewish Passover to the Jewish holiday known as Pentecost. Pentecost, like Passover, was a historically established time to celebrate. This was the time for the Jewish people to thank God for the first harvest of grain that would take place fifty days after Passover. God has often displayed that He uses these special days in fulfilling the events of Christ. As we learned earlier, it was prophesied that when this New Covenant would occur, God's law would go from being recorded on a tablet of stone, like the Ten Commandments, to being written on the hearts and minds of people (Jeremiah 31:33). Before Jesus died, He told the disciples several times it was good that He would be going away (see John chapters 14-15), because when He did, He promised to send the *Counselor*, who is one and the same as the Holy Spirit, who would both be in, and guide, all who believe. So, after forty days of resurrection visits, Jesus finally ascended into Heaven. Just before He ascended, Jesus told the apostles to wait in Jerusalem for the coming of His Holy Spirit. And the day it came was fifty days after His death on Passover, on the Jewish holiday of Pentecost.

When the Spirit of God came, people changed. Even the disciples, who prior to Pentecost even went back to fishing, after Pentecost are fueled with courage, conviction, and power. The day God ushered in this new age of the Spirit, some amazing things happened. People were speaking in foreign tongues and even flames of fire appeared over the believers' heads! The change was so evident and unusual that the Jewish people who saw this strange occurrence take place on Pentecost thought that these Christians were drunk (see Acts 2). This is when the apostle Peter, now with power granted from on high, regains his confidence and gives a profound message. Peter's message has such an amazing impact that several thousand people respond and are immediately baptized (Acts 2:36-41)! So with this kind of impact, what was it that Peter said that triggered such a response? Peter, in his message, makes reference to signs that the Jews themselves have seen, and then he brings it all together to show them that God both foretold and was behind it all. One of the things Peter did on this day was take them back to the Old Testament prophet Joel and show them that Joel foretold what is and has taken place. Here is what Peter quoted from Joel:

"And in the last days it shall be, God declares, that I will pour out my Spirit on all flesh, and your sons and your daughters shall prophesy, and your young men shall see visions, and your old men shall dream dreams; even on my male servants and female servants in those days I will pour out my Spirit, and they shall prophesy. And I will show wonders in heavens above and signs on the earth below, blood, and fire, and vapor of smoke; the sun shall be turned to darkness and the moon to blood, before the day the Lord comes, the great and magnificent day. And it shall come to pass that everyone who calls upon the name of the Lord shall be saved."

(ACTS 2:17-21, QUOTING JOEL 2:28-32, ESV)

Peter then goes on to tell the people:

"Men of Israel, hear these words: Jesus of Nazareth, a man attested to you by God with mighty works and wonders and signs that God did through him in your midst as you yourselves know—..."

(ACTS 2:22, ESV)

Peter is reminding them and saying: Don't be surprised by what you are now seeing in these people, given them through the Holy Spirit. Joel said it would come, and look at all the "mighty works, wonders, and signs that God did through Him in your midst, as you yourselves know." So besides the fact that people are speaking in foreign tongues by the aid of the Holy Spirit, what else could Peter be referring to that the people listening to him would be able to identify with, that they have already seen for themselves? The two most profound things would be that Joel prophesied the sun would be darkened and the moon turned to blood. We have already seen that, at Jesus' death, the sun was darkened. This alone would be incredible to the people! After all, the sun being darkened, during the day, would be an incredibly rare and attention-getting occurrence. The fact that this happened at the death of Jesus, as God said it would, is amazing. But there is more. What about this *moon turning to blood?* Could Peter be saying: "Hey, you have seen the blood moon, another prophecy that Joel said would happen. Since you have seen both the sun darkened and the moon turned to blood, don't doubt, but believe"? Now remember the result of Peter's message. When Peter gets done sharing his message, thousands believe and are baptized. So something Peter says, and the evidence that is gleaned from it, helps these people be convinced that his words must be true. Could the blood moon have something to do with it?

So, just what is a blood moon? A blood moon is what is known as a lunar eclipse. A lunar eclipse is a rare occurrence. It takes place, on average, in any given region, only about once per year. A lunar eclipse occurs when the earth gets in between the sun and the moon and, therefore, the moon is in the shadow of earth. When the moon is in that shadow, it looks blood red. That is why it is called a blood moon.

In order to see this evidence in its grandeur, we need to first go back and correctly justify the likely date of Jesus' death on the cross. I marvel that this can be done, as we will see, and with pretty strong certainty! To establish this we need to examine the evidence. We have already seen that Jesus died on Passover, which is remarkable since it is only one day in 365 days, a mere .27 percent of a probability. The Scriptures are also clear that Jesus died on a Friday. We know this for various reasons, but you may recall that Pilate wanted the bodies taken down from the cross before the Sabbath, which is a Saturday. (This is also why the day of Jesus' death is known as Good Friday.) We have also learned that the Passover takes place on Nissan 14, the first month of the Jewish year, and each and every year on that fourteenth day of that month. So then, if we go back in time, and inspect the calendar, can we discover whether there was a Passover, which took place on a Friday, around the suspected year of Jesus' death? As has been indicated by our prior research, we believe Jesus was born around the turn of 2 to 1 B.C., both due to the evidence regarding King Herod's death and the very rare conjunction that occurred in the sky, during that time, between planets of Venus and Jupiter. You will recall that we learned earlier that it is likely that those two planets, already the brightest two objects in the sky, when they came just seconds apart, had a role in the announcement of Jesus' birth. We have also already learned that Luke records Jesus started His ministry around the age of 30, and then we know He was present at three Passovers during His time of ministry, which would indicate a ministry period of about three years. With this evidence, the time frame of our search is around the early 30s A.D. So then, going back in the calendar to the 30s, A.D., was there a Friday that was also a Passover? In fact, there were two. The best two options for Jesus' death on a cross are Passover Friday, April 7, 30 A.D., or Friday, April 3, 33 A.D. Friday. The latter lines up best with a birth that would have occurred around the 2, to 1, B.C. time frame, Jesus being 30 years of age at the start of His ministry, and then dying three Passovers later. (Remember, there is no year 0.) Now equipped with all of this, Friday, April 3, 33 A.D. is a great choice.

So then, with this date in hand, is it possible that anything else happened on this special day to confirm not only the date, but also reveal something truly amazing? If on that special Friday of Passover, God not only darkened the sun, but also perfectly timed a lunar eclipse, just at the right time to proclaim the sacrifice of His Son, it surely would be a grand miracle. I mean, God would be showing off! If it did occur that way, God would be displaying that He inspires the words of the Bible, because the prophet Joel said all of this would happen hundreds of years earlier. If all this is true, it would be completely astonishing. And if it is true, perhaps that is why thousands of people responded to Peter's message. Which is exactly what happened.

So, how can we know if this is true
when it happened two thousand years ago?

As we have learned, with modern technology we can go back in time and put the earth, moon and sun the way they were on any day, including *that day*, with precision. So if we go back to April 3, 33 A.D., what we will find? In order to do this research, we will gain some assistance from astronomers at NASA (National Aeronautics and Space Administration). NASA should be a pretty good source for this kind of thing! It is truly incredible to see this for ourselves. This truly gives me spiritual awe. On April 3, 33 A.D., at 5:38 p.m., as could be seen from Jerusalem, there was indeed a lunar eclipse! If you want to see it for yourself go to NASA's website at the links below.

http://eclipse.gsfc.nasa.gov/5MCLEmap/0001-0100/LE0033-04-03P.gif

http://eclipse.gsfc.nasa.gov/JLEX/JLEX-AS.html

Just perceive the timing of this and all that God orchestrated in the death of His Son. He had to get Pilate and the Jewish leaders to act to have Jesus killed on that one special day, Passover. And it occurred. He worked in the soldiers' breaking the legs of the thieves but *not* the breaking of Jesus' legs, because He was the Passover Lamb, and any Passover lamb is not to have its bones broken. He worked in the soldier with the spear to make sure Jesus was pierced for our transgressions despite the fact neither of the thieves were pierced. On top of all of this, the sun was darkened and, incredibly, as can be shown, on the very day of Jesus' death, God lines up the sun, earth, and moon to create a lunar eclipse, fulfilling Joel's prophecy that the moon would turn to blood![15] The odds of all of this happening, just as was foretold hundreds of years earlier, is astronomical. Furthermore, we know it all was foretold due to the discovery of the Dead Sea Scrolls.

What is the larger point? God is real, He has a plan, His Word can be trusted, His Bible can be trusted, Jesus can be trusted as the Lamb of God, and as a result we can believe in God and the sacrifice of His Son Jesus Christ as our Savior and Lord. There is so much evidence showing us that Jesus and the Bible are true; now the question becomes whether we will allow Jesus and the Bible to guide our lives. All of this begs a response. Here is a great question: Knowing what God has done for us through his Son, Jesus, and the evidence that is left to convince us this is true, what is the proper response that He desires from us? That is a question we will see answered through an inspiring story in our next dramatic chapter.

Before getting to it, however, we need to understand the significance of the New Covenant age, which began in full measure on Pentecost. We now live in the age of the Holy Spirit.

The Cross Allowed God to Come Near at Pentecost

In following the story of God's people, we have seen their immense struggle with sin and how that sin separated man from God. When Adam and Eve sinned in the garden, they were removed from the garden and from the close presence of God. Later, in the desert, at the tabernacle, God made a way for man to come near through lambs offered as sacrifices. That forgiveness, however, was temporary. Although God came nearer through the tabernacle, the relationship was not like it was in the garden. But God foretold by the prophets that one day He would make a New Covenant and that His laws would be in our hearts and minds. Man, ever since the garden, has been told repeatedly by God to multiply the image and likeness of God. Yet man did not have a full picture of what God was like. When man needed a further revelation of who God was, so that we could know more about Him, He came to earth through Jesus, Immanuel, God with us. Since the advent of Jesus we know so much more about what

God is like and what He desires of us. However, when Jesus was here, He was both God and man. Due to this, Jesus was temporarily limited by time and space. If you did not live in Galilee or Jerusalem, you would not see Jesus, nor sense His spiritual presence. Prior to this time, in the Old Testament, God allowed special people at special times to sense His Spirit, but the Spirit of God was not with or in every man who believed in Him. After Jesus died on a cross, as the final Lamb of God who takes away the sins of the world, the sin that separated us from God is forgiven through faith. The sin that separated a holy God from sinful man was now dealt with, allowing God's presence to come near man again. Fifty days after the cross on Pentecost, now with a solution for our sin problem, God could send his Holy Spirit to be with all who believe, and to have that Spirit without limitation. The common man is now able to have the closest relationship to God possible, since the garden, because the sin of believers has been dealt with. This Holy Spirit is available to anyone, anywhere, at anytime, to any and all who believe. Prior to believing, however, the Spirit cannot be in us because our sin is still in the way. When that's the case, we struggle without the aid of His Holy Spirit to help us. We need the Holy Spirit to become the people He wants us to be. This is why Jesus said, while he was still alive:

**"Nevertheless, I tell you the truth: it is to your advantage that
I go away, for if I do not go away, the Helper will not come to you.
But if I go, I will send him to you."**

(JOHN 16:7, ESV)

This is an awesome privilege and blesses our lives as we stay intimately connected to Him. Sadly, many times we don't sense God's presence, not because He is not there, but because we do not seek Him as we should. Our busyness and our focus on other things chokes us out from sensing the presence of God. That is not His desire! When we believe in Jesus as Lord, we get many gifts wrapped in one present. The gifts include forgiveness of sin, the guidance of the Holy Spirit, and eternal life. These are the best gifts of all. These gifts are offered to us by God when we respond to Him with faith.

This Holy Spirit is available to anyone, anywhere, at any time, to any and all who believe.

When I became a believer, instantly God began to do a work in me that He is still doing today through this Holy Spirit. The Bible teaches us that the Holy Spirit comes to be with us, guide us, convict and prune us, teach us, and empower us. Throughout my walk as a Christian I have experienced all of these. God, who wants us to multiply His image and likeness, has now provided a Helper, a Counselor—His Holy Spirit—to aid us in both becoming more like Him and bearing fruit in the lives of others.

When Peter closed his message on that very first Pentecost of the New Covenant era, he said:

And Peter said to them, "Repent and be baptized, every one of you, in the name of Jesus Christ for the forgiveness of your sins, and you will receive the gift of the Holy Spirit."

(ACTS 2:38, ESV)

The same is true today. God provided the once and final sacrifice for sin so that everyone who believes in Him would receive the forgiveness of sins and the gift of the Holy Spirit. One day the direct presence of God will be fully restored, just as it was in the garden. Until that time we have the awesome privilege of the presence of God's Holy Spirit to be with us until we receive our eternal home. We must always honor that on the Passover Jesus endured the cross. And it is through the cross that we received God's Holy Spirit at Pentecost.

Discussion Questions

**Two experiences helped the disciples
be willing to *altar* their lives
to spread the Gospel of Jesus Christ.
They are Jesus' resurrection and Pentecost.**

1) Why do you think the resurrection visits were so important to the faith of the disciples? How do you think it impacted the way they lived their lives?

2) What is Pentecost from an Old Testament perspective? (See Exodus 16:9-12.)

3) What happened on the first Pentecost after the death of Christ on Passover? You may want to read all or portions of Acts 2 describing this special day.

4) Do you, and *why* do you (if so), find it interesting that God had His Son die on Passover and His Spirit come on Pentecost? How could this build our faith?

5) What is a lunar eclipse?

6) Describe the significance of Joel's prophecy and what happened on Passover Friday, April 3, 33 A.D.?

7) How does this evidence, when combined with all of the other fulfilled prophecies, impact your view of the reliability of the Bible?

8) What is the gift given to any true believer that began in earnest on Pentecost? (See Acts 2:38.) What is having this gift like? If you have, describe how you have experienced the Holy Spirit?

Chapter Fifteen
. . . .

Have You **Altar'd** Your Life?
Making It Personal

The events of the early church, after the death and resurrection of Jesus, are written in the Acts of the Apostles, better known as the biblical book of Acts. Acts records the events of the apostles and early Christian church for the next thirty years. Shortly after the book's author, Luke, finishes his recording of Acts, Peter and Paul are martyred for their courageous leadership in spreading Christianity. This Paul was a Jewish Pharisee who, after Jesus' death, was doing everything he could to stop the advance of Christianity. He received permission to take Christians to prison and even gave his approval of the stoning of one Christian leader (Stephen) to death. One day, Jesus sees Paul from Heaven, and Jesus appears to want Paul's zeal on the right team—His team. This Paul had a great deal of zeal; it was just misdirected. As Paul is walking along the road on his crusade against Christians, Jesus appears to him in a bright light, speaks to him, blinds him for a few days, and then sets up a meeting between Paul and a follower of Jesus, who ends up praying for him. Through this prayer the power of God heals Paul so that his sight is restored. What an amazing story! (See Acts 9.)

What makes this event so tremendous is that, afterward, Paul lives a radically transformed life. Paul immediately converts from being a Jewish Pharisee who is trying to take out Christianity to becoming, in my estimation, the number one missionary of all time. He tirelessly travels throughout the region from Italy to Jerusalem on multiple occasions, plants churches, preaches the Gospel, is thrown in jail, beaten, stoned, shipwrecked, and yet his resolve to continue the mission is unshaken. How can one go from killing Christians to being a missionary for the Christian faith—unless God changes them? One of things that is so amazing about God, and offers another compelling reason to believe, is His ability to transform a person's life. The cool thing about this type of evidence is that many times we get to see this change in someone's life, lived out before us. I have seen God make such dramatic changes in my life, and in the lives of so many others. I am thankful to God for His power to change lives.

While Paul was traveling about as a missionary, he wrote many letters to various churches that he ministered to, or to Christians in cities that he desired to minister in one day. Many of these letters are woven into what is now the New Testament. The most thorough and theologically advanced letter Paul wrote is his letter to Christians in Rome. It is best known as Romans. In Romans, Paul illustrates the history of God's dealings and message to His people. He thoroughly displays that sin has created a barrier in our relationship with God and that man needs a solution to this problem. You may recall some of these rock solid statements from Paul, contained in Romans, which help clarify the Gospel of Jesus Christ.

...for all have sinned and fall short of the glory of God,
and are justified by his grace as a gift,
through the redemption that is in Christ Jesus,
whom God put forward as a propitiation
by his blood to be received by faith.

(ROMANS 3:23-25a, ESV)

...but God shows his love for us
in that while we were still sinners,
Christ died for us.

(ROMANS 5:8, ESV)

For the wages of sin is death,
but the free gift of God is eternal life
in Christ Jesus our Lord.

(ROMANS 6:23, ESV)

Romans is the longest letter of Paul's writings and includes sixteen chapters. For the first eleven chapters Paul systematically conveys a powerful gospel message. Toward the end of those eleven chapters Paul is nearing the end of his argument and therefore is about to deliver the "now what." If it were a movie, he would be at the climax. And Romans 12:1 is the pinnacle. It is the place where he states: as a result of everything I have said, this is the proper response. This is the "what we are to do about it."

Paul, at the end of chapter 11, works up to his most pivotal statement by first stating:

For God has consigned all to disobedience
that he may have mercy on them all.

(ROMANS 11:32, ESV)

This reaffirms what Paul said previously, that all have sinned and fall short of the glory of God and are justified by grace through the blood of Christ. It follows the same theme we have displayed through the rip current illustration throughout this book. All people in this world have a sin problem and are in a rip current that pulls them away from God. None of us are strong enough to beat the current on our own. It is actually a beautiful thing that this is so. It means we need the mercy of God. And praise God that He, who is rich in mercy, provided what we need. God sent His Son to jump in the rip current that was taking our lives. He jumped in and gave us His life vest so that we could be saved, knowing that He would die in the process.

Paul is now ready to deliver the pivotal point of his letter.

I appeal to you therefore, brothers, by the mercies of God,
to present (offer) your bodies as living sacrifice,
holy and acceptable to God, which is your spiritual worship.

(ROMANS 12:1, ESV)

To put this in straightforward terms, before we get to an amazing, historic understanding of this passage, Paul is saying that our proper response is...

To offer Him our lives.

God's desire is that we would go before him and express to him what follows.

God,

knowing all You have done for me,
what would You have me do for You?
God, here I am.
I give my life to be used by You.

The title of this book is **Altar'd.** Christian, have you **Altar'd** your life? Have you presented your life back to God on His altar as a living sacrifice? Here I am, God. Use me. God desires that our response to His sacrifice would be to offer our lives to the One who first offered His.

We may need to die to ourselves, but we certainly don't have to die. Jesus died, and now wants us alive! To present ourselves to him with all of our gifts, talents, and resources and say, "God, guide my life, direct my life to be pleasing to you. You are the potter. I'll be the clay."

Paul has subtly and clearly brought into view the theme of an offering we have been discussing since the beginning. In the Old Testament, for the forgiveness of sin, an offering of a lamb would be made. As we have learned, Jesus was the Lamb of God, presented by God, as the final sacrifice for sin. In this climactic verse, Paul uses that picture, figuratively, to share with us that our proper response is to now *be* the offering. The greatest offering we can give to God is the offering of *me*. Jesus **Altar'd** His life by offering it on a cross. We altar our lives by offering our life to God, in response to the cross. This may sound scary, but when you understand God and how well He knows us, it becomes exciting.

One time I went on a mission trip to Jamaica and there was a wonderful Jamaican singer and songwriter who led us in worship. I will never forget the lyrics to one of his songs. This is what it said: *"Give him your will, because He knows you well."* God knows our interests, talents, and gifts. God is not about making our lives miserable. He loves us. We are His children. But He does want us to realign our priorities with Him so that we take pleasure in what He takes pleasure in. Once our motives are right, He can give us a great life of being used by Him in a unique and special way in line with how He created us.

Offering our lives as a living sacrifice is so true and so right, and yet many well-intentioned Christians have held back from placing their lives on God's altar. One of the reasons this may be so is because Jesus' sacrifice may have not become personal to them. This person may know the Gospel and understand it, but they may understand it outside of themselves rather than the understanding reaching the depths of their inner being.

I'd like to share a story. It is designed to help everyone experience the sacrifice of Christ in a deeply personal way.

God, please help all of us who are reading or listening to be in the present with You as we see your great sacrifice for us in a new and intimate way.

To understand this story we need to go back in time a couple of thousand years.

Imagine you are a sinner, as we all are, and you know it, but you are in a time and space of two thousand years ago. You have lied to your parents, at times you have directly disrespected them, you have stolen at least once in your life, you have used the Lord's name in vain, you have lusted, perhaps had sex outside of marriage, perhaps dozens of times—at least in your mind—you have used vulgarity, profanity, done drugs, and perhaps the worst thing is that many times you have ignored God. Certainly you have not always lived for Him the way you should.

Thankfully, God has given you a method of getting right with Him.

It's the time of year for you to go make your sacrifice and to get your sins atoned for. You are looking forward to going. You feel so distant from God and you so desperately want your sin atoned for so you can feel clean, right, and forgiven. You are looking forward to being able to draw near to God again. So you go to your animals, and since you only have a few, this is going to be costly, especially since you must pick out your best lamb. So you look them over to make sure the one you choose is without defect. You want to honor God in bringing a right sacrifice. So you pick your best and most valuable animal and begin to head toward the temple with your lamb on a lead cord. There are others on the street. This is a busy day for sacrifice. But on this day something different and unusual is taking place. As you near the temple you see some people walking away from the temple and they still have their animal. Their heads are down and you can tell something is wrong. This is confusing and upsetting to you. Why do they have their lamb with them, and why are they heading home? Others are walking away from the temple and they seem almost overwhelmed with a deep and reverential joy. Their burdens are lifted. Although people are normally walking home without a lamb, the joy these people are experiencing seems to surpass what you have seen in the past. Why is this the case? And why are some walking home downcast, but with their animal?

As you get nearer to the temple one of the priests comes and walks beside you, saying, "Sir...ma'am...you're going to have to do away with your animal. That won't work here anymore."

Huh, you are thinking. This does not make sense. "What do you mean?" you ask. "We have been doing this for nearly two thousand years."

The priest responds, "Animal sacrifices are not good anymore. God has made a new agreement. God has made a New Covenant. Animal sacrifices won't work anymore. I am sorry."

You are crushed. You're carrying this huge burden of sin and you wanted to be made right with God. To be forgiven. "No, no, don't say that," you answer. "Sir, I need to be forgiven. You don't understand. I am a sinner. I am a broken man. I need to offer this sacrifice to be right with God. Do not withhold this from me."

The priest responds, "I am sorry, but even if you were to sacrifice this animal, you would not receive forgiveness."

You are downcast, in tears, and a state of shock, as this does not make any sense to you. You don't know what to do, so you just stop on the road and stare at the ground in deep and sorrowful thought. *What am I going to do?*

After time passes, you hear another voice. "Son...daughter... why are you so downcast? Trust in God. Trust also in me."

You look up and discover that the priest's countenance has totally changed and his face shines with a beautiful, bright light. He says to you, "I am the way the truth and the life, no one comes to the Father except through me."

You are utterly in awe of what you are now seeing. It's, it's... *Jesus*...you are standing next to Jesus. You can't believe what is happening.

Jesus says, "If you are willing, let go of your animal and instead walk with me. I am about to do something incredible for you. I can make you clean, but you must believe and leave that animal behind. You must leave your old religion behind, leave your old ways behind, leave your old sin behind, and come with me.

You think to yourself that this must be why some were walking away with their animals. They were unwilling to humble themselves. They were unwilling to leave their old ways behind.

For a moment you ponder what to do. You look to Jesus, and when you do, you see someone awesome, glorious, and filled with love. You then look down to your lamb, which has been your long-standing means of forgiveness. You then look to Jesus again. He is giving you the expression that begs you to come to Him and trust Him. You then look down to your lamb and with some anxiety you slowly drop the lead and set the animal free. You have just lost control.

Jesus says, "Come, follow me." And now, instead of walking your animal, you are walking with Jesus. As you walk along you begin to wonder: *Where are we going?* You were heading for the temple, the place of sacrifice, and Jesus is following the same path.

Jesus goes on to tell you that God loves you and that He wants to forgive you, but this time, it will be once and for all. You will not have to come to this place of sacrifice again. He also tells you that God has prepared a final sacrifice, because God has not changed the rules, but rather fulfilled them. So far this sounds OK. Then Jesus says, "A sacrifice is still needed. Don't worry. You will find out soon enough."

What does that mean? You then continue walking in step with Jesus, completely in awe. Eventually you arrive at the temple gate. This is when something strange and yet familiar happens, all at the same time. Some priests come up like they normally would, to inspect your lamb for blemishes, and you look to Jesus as though to say to Him: I don't have my lamb, because I let it go, as you said. The priests walk right by you as though you don't matter and, while Jesus stands still, the priests walk around Him and begin to closely inspect Him! At first, you don't know what to make of this, but you are already beginning to have a nervous reaction. Then a knot forms in your stomach, and your face turns pale.

Then, just as a lamb would be given a seal indicating it had passed inspection, the priests proclaim out loud, in your hearing: "Yes, all is perfect. This is an acceptable sacrifice."

You start panicking. What is going on here? See, you have done this before. Now you are starting to see what is happening and you cannot bear it. They just inspected Jesus. You are starting to freak out. You were walking a lamb and then you walked with Jesus. Normally, your lamb would be inspected, and now they were inspecting Jesus. The next thing that always occurred in the past was that you then sacrificed your lamb. "This can't be," you find yourself saying. "Jesus, this can't be. I can't do this."

Jesus, knowing you now understand what is taking place, looks at you and says, "Come with me to the place of sacrifice."

You start to get emotional. Tears are falling down your face. "Jesus, I can't do this. I can't."

Jesus says, "You must. Your sin must be paid for."

"Then let me," you say. "Let me pay for it!"

Jesus says, "You don't want to do that. If you pay for your sin, it will be forever in a place you don't want to go. This is God's plan for me. It's OK. I am willing to die for your sin because I love you with the Father's love."

"Jesus, how can I do this?" you say.

"You must," Jesus says. "It is time. You have to make a decision. ...But you do have a choice.

"You can pay for your sin forever in Hell, or you can allow me to pay for your sin, and you will be forgiven. I tell you with those words because I love you and so desperately don't want you to go there. I came to restore your relationship with God now and forever! Please allow me to give you what I desire: life eternal and life abundantly.

Jesus looks you directly in the eyes, with eyes full of love, and tells you, "The time of sacrifice has come." You cannot believe what is happening. This is so incredibly hard. But then it becomes even harder. Jesus bends down on His hands and feet in the posture of a lamb, because He is the Lamb of God.

The priest at the temple gate says, "Come on, we don't have all day. Put your hand on your sacrifice, take this knife, and sacrifice God's Lamb."

You can't believe this is happening. All of these years that you brought your own sacrifices, often you were just going through the motions. Not this time; this time it is so real, it as though time has stopped and you can hear every beat of your heart.

"Jesus, how can I do this?" you say.

Jesus answers: "You must. Someone must pay for your sin. Without sacrifice, without blood, sin is not forgiven. My Father required fifteen hundred years of sacrifice. The lamb always had to shed blood for sins to be forgiven. *I* am the final Lamb. I am *your* final Lamb. If you will believe in me."

Jesus continues: "I know, my child, that this is hard. But it is supposed to be. In this way you are seeing what I have done for you, *personally*. God the Father and I love you so much, and we desire your full devotion. We are giving you this experience so that you will remember what we have done for you. Now you must get on with this; there are others waiting. Put your hand on my head."

The hand on the head is just like the sacrifice of the lamb at the tabernacle. In this way you identify with the lamb's sacrifice for you. In this way your sin is put on the lamb as a substitute. In this way you feel the lamb die for you. You are about to feel Jesus die for your personal sin. The method of sacrifice is a knife across the throat. When a lamb would quiver at its death, you would *feel* the death of the lamb under your hand.

Oh, how this makes all the difference when we experience Jesus dying for our sin. Not just the world's sin, but *my* sin. That our sins put him on that cross. It is our sin that nailed Him there, but it was His love that kept Him there.

So you put your hand on Jesus, and after He makes eye contact with you one last time, with eyes of love and compassion, with one swift wave of the knife, you sacrifice Jesus.

You stand there in awe. You are shaken. At this moment you can't help but be downcast as Jesus lays dead before you. *How could I do this? How could I kill Jesus?*

And that is exactly what we did. All of us.

As you stand there deeply saddened, a priest whispers to you. "Don't be so downcast. Easter is coming. Jesus knew He was going to die, and He also knew He would rise again. Jesus has victory over death, and now you will one day too." It takes a moment for this to sink in. Slowly you begin to get it. A sense of hope begins to sweep over you, and your frown begins to turn around. You begin to get it. A huge burden has been lifted. This was God's plan, and God will raise Him from death. You will never make another animal sacrifice. You have been forgiven once and for all! A weight has been lifted from your shoulders. You have been promised not only forgiveness of sin, but eternal life. You have been made clean. Hallelujah. Jesus is going to rise from the dead. Sunday's coming!

Worthy is the Lamb who has been slain. The love of Jesus, the love of God, has saved me!

Oh, the mercy of God. Oh God, thank you for what Jesus did for me. I am so thankful.

This story is shared as a means of helping Jesus' sacrifice become more personal. You likely recall that Thomas and the apostles were able to see and even touch the holes in Jesus' hands, feet, and side during a couple of Jesus' resurrection visits. Can you imagine the appreciation that would flood your being if you were to see and touch His scars? Did you know this may very well occur? Toward the end of the apostle John's life, Jesus gives John a revelation of what will take place one day in Heaven.

John, in chapter 5 of Revelation, conveys to us a heavenly scene. The Father, God, is on the throne and a sealed scroll is in His right hand, but no one is found worthy to open the scroll and look into it. John gets rather emotional about this, even to the point of tears. He deeply wants to know the words of God written in the scroll. And then:

And one of the elders said to me [John],

"Weep no more, behold, the Lion of the tribe of Judah,

the Root of David, has conquered,

so that he can open the scroll and its seven seals."

And between the throne and the four living creatures

and among the elders

<u>I saw a Lamb standing, as though it had been slain,</u>

with seven horns and with seven eyes, which are the seven spirits

of God sent out into the earth. And [he] took the scroll from the

right hand of him who was seated on the throne.

And when he had taken the scroll,

the four living creatures and the twenty-four elders

fell down before the Lamb, each holding a harp,

and golden bowls full of incense,

which are the prayers of the saints.

And they sang a new song saying,

"Worthy are you to take the scroll and to open its seals,

for you were slain, and by your blood

you ransomed people for God

from every tribe and language and people and nation,

and you have made them a kingdom of priests
to our God, and they shall reign on earth."
Then I looked, and I heard around the throne
and the living creatures and the elders
the voice of many angels, numbering myriads of myriads
and thousands of thousands, saying with a loud voice,
Worthy is the Lamb who was slain, to receive power
and wealth and wisdom and might
and honor and glory and blessing!"
And I heard every creature in heaven
and on earth and under the earth and in the sea
and all that is in them, saying,
"To him who sits on the throne and to the Lamb
be blessings and honor and glory and might forever and ever!"
And the four living creatures said, "Amen!"
and the elders fell down and worshipped.

(JOHN 5:5-14, ESV)

Can you imagine the day we see Jesus' scars, face-to-face? It is beneficial for us to imagine, with grand anticipation, of the day that we see the Lamb standing, as though it had been slain. Seeing Jesus' sacrifice for you and me in a very personal way compels us to **Altar** our lives to the one who first **Altar'd** His. Have you **Altar'd** your life before the Lamb? He gave His all and is worthy of ours. In the chapters to come we will learn what it means to **Altar** our lives and how, as a result, our lives can be so much more purposeful.

Discussion Questions

1) What can you share about the book of Romans in general, and then the emphasis leading up to Romans 12:1?

2) What impacted you about the drama? How does it help you identify more deeply with what Jesus Christ did for you?

3) How do you think it would impact you to see the scar marks of Jesus one day in Heaven?

4) What does Romans 12:1 mean, and how does it compare to our theme of an offering used throughout this book? What would it mean to offer yourself as a living sacrifice to God?

Chapter Sixteen

What It Means to Be Altar'd

Have you **Altar'd** your life before the one who first offered His? What would it mean to offer our all to the One who first offered His?

Before any person is willing to offer their life to Jesus, he or she needs to believe He is worthy. In order to realize the magnitude of His worthiness, a person needs to fully comprehend what he has done for them.

You may recall that early in Jesus' ministry His mother and brothers were trying to take charge of Jesus and help him to be more, we might say, reasonable. When He began announcing that He was the promised One to come, at first they did not know what to make of it. His brothers were not instant followers, but in the end they became convinced that Jesus was Lord. In fact, Jesus' brothers James and Jude ended up writing books of the Bible titled after their names. They, like everyone else close to Him after the resurrection, became convinced that he was Lord. That encourages me and I hope it does you, too.

In Jude's biblical letter he closes with some remarkable words. When fully comprehended, they help us grasp what Jesus did for us.

Now to him who is able to keep you from stumbling and to present you blameless before the presence of his glory with great joy, to the only true God, our Savior, through Jesus Christ our Lord, be glory, majesty, dominion, and authority, before all time and now and forever. Amen.

(JUDE 24, 25, ESV)

What an amazing thing to say. The first part of this passage reminds me that, now with the aid of the Holy Spirit, we have a helper to keep us from stumbling—from falling, constantly, like those Israelites that we read about. We are not fooling God; indeed, we still are not without sin. Although we are not sinless, we now are strengthened to *sin less.* His Counselor is a great helper for us. As we continue to set our minds on Christ, we can much better maintain His perspective. As great as it is that He helps us from living life in a constant stumble, it is the next thing Jude writes that we need to truly appreciate.

Jude writes that we will one day be presented before God's presence, blameless in His glory, with great joy! It would be helpful for us to envision this heavenly scene. We are about to dig into what it would mean to **Altar** our lives while we are on earth. This is good and right. But what is so compelling and awesome is the assurance that one day, as a result, we will be before God on the altar of Heaven, and we will be deemed blameless in the presence of His glory, with great joy. The Bible indicates that there is a *Bema seat* (judgment seat) in Heaven, one that is there even for us believers! What is so amazing is that, due to our faith in Jesus, our Passover Lamb, when we are before God, in that glorious moment, we will be found blameless! It is not that we are perfect or without blame. It is that Christ has given His believers His righteousness that comes from being perfectly forgiven. When we realize that Jesus **Altar'd** His life on the cross in order to present us blameless before God, we are compelled to offer Him our lives in gratitude to the One who first offered His.

So then, it almost appears that the judgment seat is without judgment. That, however, is not true. The judgment will not be regarding a penalty for sin. Jesus took care of that. The judgment is more about what you do with your life knowing all that Jesus first did for you. How we altered our lives to live for Him. This judgment has much more to do with our reward. The Bible is clear that there are heavenly rewards for living your life for God's mission. God's mission has been made clear throughout the Bible and through this book. We are to bear the image of God and be fruitful and multiply His followers throughout the nations. God wants us to partner with Him in teaching His ways to others, thereby helping others to become more like Him and to do likewise. The heavenly judgment that awaits us will impact our reward and be based on our willingness and engagement in **altaring**—and altering—our lives to serve His Kingdom by living to bear fruit. This is what Paul meant in one of our theme verses.

> I appeal to you therefore, brothers, by the mercies of God,
> to present [offer] your bodies as a living sacrifice,
> holy and acceptable to God, which is your spiritual worship.
>
> (ROMANS 12:1, ESV)

The general will of God for all of us is to **altar** (offer) Him our lives. Here is a great prayer to do just that. If you and/or you and some fellow disciples are ready to do this, I would encourage you to set up a memorable time to kneel before God, be still before Him, and offer your life to Him. I think it would be great to find your own special, memorable place, whether it be at your home or in a special outdoor spot (like the cover photo to this book) to do this. God many times uses mountaintops or hilltops for special experiences! Even as we read, when Abraham offered Isaac, and God redeemed Isaac with an animal sacrifice, it all took place on a mountaintop. Although you don't need to do this with anyone but God to be legit, wouldn't it be cool for a small group of people to offer their lives together and continue to encourage each other in living for God more fully? So here is a simple prayer you may want to say to God to offer your life to Him.

God,

I trust You. I believe in You. I am grateful for all that You have done through Your Son. I offer my life to be used by You. Here I am. Take my life. Use and direct my life for Your glory.

Give Him your will;
remember, He knows you well.

The beautiful thing is that offering our lives to God is the same for all of us generally, and then the result of doing so is very different for each of us specifically. What do I mean? The act of surrendering to God and saying, "God, I am yours, please guide me to your will," is the same for all of us. However, what God will do with each of our lives, specifically, is very unique. We tend to like the latter and struggle more with the former! Before I move on, however, I cannot stress enough how important it is that we trust God by offering to Him our lives as a living sacrifice. If and when you do that, you can know that God is tremendously pleased. As Romans 12:1 says,

I appeal to you therefore, brothers, by the mercies of God, to present (offer) your bodies as a living sacrifice, holy and acceptable to God, which is your spiritual worship.

(ROMANS 12:1 ESV)

Some may say feel like they have already done this, or now are willing to do so, but they still don't know what God wants to do with their life. My advice would be to first make sure you know God's pleasure in your willingness to offer your life! We must also keep in mind God's mission to multiply His followers around the world. If you have both of these things in mind, and you don't know specifically what to do, there may be a very good reason. God may not yet have revealed it to you! Which means: relax. Follow God, grow in Him, follow His general will, trust Him, and wait for what God has planned for you. If you have offered your life, He is already pleased! The call of God to offer our lives to Him is *now*. The specifics of what that will mean, and when, is up to God. The important thing is that we continue to place our personal lump of clay on His potter's wheel and allow Him to create something beautiful and useable for His intended purposes. With God you can be assured it will be! And I believe, in most instances, it will also be something you are very excited to do.

So then, what may His specific will look like for your life? Never forget what God wants. In the first command God said: I created you to be in my image and likeness; be fruitful and multiply. In some of Jesus' very last words on earth He said something very similar. "Go make disciples of all nations, baptizing them in the name of the Father, Son and Holy Spirit and teaching them to obey everything I have commanded you" (Matthew 28:18, ESV). A disciple is someone who follows after the teaching of another. Jesus was the image and likeness of God, and He asked people to follow Him, and then, when trained, He asked them to go make more disciples who would follow His teachings. The first and last mission statements of

God go hand in hand. But then, there is the question I am sure you want answered: *How do I apply this to my own life?*

I look forward to sharing some exciting examples. The applications can be very different for each of us.

I love the game of golf and am an avid fan. I really admire Tiger Woods for all that he has accomplished on a golf course. I know he has also done some great things with his foundation, but what really amazes me is how focused, committed, and dominant he has been on the golf course. As I write, he has not been performing like he did just a few short years ago, but I anticipate he will be great again. Some people have given me some flack as a pastor, to also be a Tiger Woods fan. He definitely has incurred his share of struggles off the course. I try not to judge people who have had a completely different background than me. If I grew up in the poor inner city, or became unbelievably wealthy like Tiger Woods, could I be certain I would not have made some of the mistakes he made? I know that, for me, without a close relationship with God, I am more susceptible to falling. So what is my purpose in bringing up Tiger Woods? I can't help but get excited about the kind of impact Tiger could make on our world as a sold-out believer for Jesus Christ. What if he sought Jesus, found him, became a born-again believer, and **Altar'd** his life before God? What could that look like, and what kind of impact could he have? I guess God could call him to be a missionary. But you know what I think God may do? Call him to be a Christian golfer. One whose desire for golf is second to his desire to be fruitful and multiply followers of Jesus. Tiger would likely be able to do more good through his golf platform than many other forms of ministry. What if he spoke to young people, and for that matter any people, nearly weekly on his tour stops? People would flock to hear what he had to say, especially as his life transformed before us. What if what he shared on these tour stops was a testimony about how God transformed his life through the Gospel of Jesus Christ, and the help of the Holy Spirit, which had now given him strength to overcome temptation, and even better yet, live a purposeful life? I can't help but get happy just simply thinking about this! I have at times felt led to write him a letter and see if I could meet with him. Perhaps this is that letter. I would love for him, and the world, to see the evidence for Jesus being the Lamb of God who takes away the sins of the world, and to place their faith and life in His hands.

Another example along a similar line of thought is my daughter, who happens to be on the cover of this book. My daughter has developed an interest in the game of golf. If I had more room in this book, I could tell you about our road trip to the famous Masters golf tournament with a tent, a Chevy, and no tickets—and how we got in to the Masters to watch three days of the best in the world playing the game! Since then, she has fallen in love with the game and is starting to get good at playing it. Her goal is to seek a Division I college scholarship. Abby and I love to talk golf and work on our games.

How does one manage this love and interest with the call of God to **Altar** his or her life? Keeping God and his purposes number one needs to be the first priority for all of us. So how do we attempt to do this, and do this well? On the way to the course, many times Abby and I do Bible devotions or talk about God and our priorities. I encourage her to keep up her personal devotions and relationship with Him. She is active in church, youth group, and summer spiritual camps. As much as we love the game, we always talk about keeping God and His mission first. We also talk about the purpose of golf in her life. If golf is about her and her success, then it is not an **Altar'd** life. Abby, like all of us, needs to put her lump of clay on His wheel and allow Him to make something beautiful and useful for His Kingdom. We have talked about how she may be able to use her golf platform with the other younger golfers in her program, and how she may be able to use it in the future to speak into the hearts of many about where her true purpose and strength comes from. For Abby, as long as she has placed herself on God's altar, and allows Him to direct her life, it is always going to be great. Whether He uses golf or not is not of utmost importance. Offering her life to Him, however He chooses to use it to bear fruit in the lives of others...this is her call, as it is the call for each of us. God may choose to use her sport as a means of ministry. God may one day ask her to lay it down to serve him in a different manner. The point is, wherever you are now in your life, use it as your platform to serve God's Kingdom purposes. In addition, regularly seek God, be still before Him, put your clay on His wheel, and allow Him to affirm or redirect your path.

In my life, God called me from an eleven-year real estate and development career into full-time ministry. I am continually amazed how God will call you to something that He gives you the desire for. I don't think most people have to serve God kicking and screaming. I really believe that when you place your lump of clay on His altar, He will shape you and give you the proper desire to be used. It is fun to do something we are designed to do well. Trust God. He has a good plan for you! As my Jamaican friend sings, "Give him your will, because he knows you well."

All of this in no way means that it is easy. I have been in ministry for eleven years, and those eleven were far more fruitful for God's Kingdom than the previous eleven, but they have also been, in many ways, harder. Our finances are significantly more challenging than they were eleven years ago, but I would not trade these last eleven years! Although we still are in our journey of becoming more like Him, my wife, kids, and I are much better off in our relationship with God than we would have been. In addition, we have experienced hardship which God has used to develop our character. Some of you, God may indeed be asking, to make a radical change. Perhaps as you **Altar** your life before Him, He will call you to be a pastor, or missionary, or take over a women's ministry, or become a youth pastor. However big that change may be, listen to Him, trust Him, and follow Him. I believe He will give you the desire for what He calls you to. If God is calling you to ministry, you need to respond to Him, but it is wise to do so while counting the cost. Always remember that the cost God paid in sacrificing His Son was large. But He planned for it. There will be a cost and sacrifice that goes into serving God vocationally. Count it, but do it anyway, knowing He is worthy.

Some of you may not sense the call to full-time vocational ministry and may still be wondering what your **Altar'd** life might look like. I can't stress enough this next question. Have you truly knelt before God and said, "God, I offer you my life?" Assuming you have, for some, it may not be that He changes your vocation, but rather your purpose in your vocation. He may take your life and say, "You know what, I want you to be a mom and raise your kids to know and follow after me. I want you to grow so deep in your own relationship with me that it spills over onto your kids. Your full-time ministry begins with your family. Make your parenting intentional in raising up followers of me!"

God may take businessmen and make them fishers of men. These men and women can then be awesome examples and witnesses in the workplace. Your pastor is not in that place; you are! He wants all business people to be men or women of integrity, men and women who have a purpose greater than business.

> **God cares more about people**
> **knowing Him than he does about that business.**
> **Make sure you do too.**

Perhaps you can start a lunch or breakfast Bible study, or invite others to a Bible study that you already attend. Make a priority of going out with people to lunch to encourage them in their lives and faith.

God's altar, for many people, is not a change in surroundings, but rather having them change the way they see and minister to what already surrounds them.

Realign your purpose in your surroundings and perhaps your **Altar'd** purpose will be serving God where He already has you. This is definitely true for many, but make sure it's not lip service. Make it your consuming passion to be bear fruit where you are planted. Spend time thinking about this. Ask others for advice on how you could do this. Make a strategic plan on how you can use your time to be more effective.

My wife is a public school teacher who is not free to be a vocal witness for her faith. However, she shares her faith through her love for the kids. She shares her faith by how she treats them and helps them to succeed in their education and life. She invites people to church when she can. People see Christ in her. On top of that, she carries the family health insurance and helps provide a stable income so her husband can give his life to serve God's Kingdom. On top of all of this, she raises her kids with amazing skill. It will be interesting to see how God continues to use her, but I believe she is doing what God has for her in the now. She, like the rest of us, from time to time needs to re-place herself before God on His potter's wheel.

May we all continue to be open to how God can direct our future. As our kids move out of the house, perhaps God has something new for my wife, or myself, and perhaps God has something new for you. It is awesome and wise to place ourselves before Him with humble hearts, knowing that it is never too late for God to realign us to His will. A new season of life may be a great time to revisit the altar. Even if you already *have* **Altar'd** your life. Consider setting up a special time with God to do it again, and let God know you want to allow Him to redirect your life if He were to so choose. Trust Him that He has great plans for you! He knows how to work your clay, and He will shape you in a special way so that you can use the gifts He has already given you.

In the end, our new life begins at the altar, before God. Jesus offered His all. In one of the most profound statements of the Bible, we are asked to offer ours.

> **I appeal to you therefore, brothers,**
>
> **by the mercies of God,**
>
> **to present [offer] your bodies as a living sacrifice,**
>
> **holy and acceptable to God,**
>
> **which is your spiritual worship.**
>
> (ROMANS 12:1, ESV)

Discussion Questions
....

1) How would you describe what it looks like to offer (**Altar**) one's life to God?

2) Share with each other whether you have truly taken the time and humbled yourself before God to offer (**Altar**) your life? If yes, what was this like? How did it change your life? If not, what is holding you back?

3) What do the following song lyrics mean to you? "Give him your will, because he knows you well." Even though these are lyrics and not a Bible verse, what do you think of their truthfulness? Do you think most of the time God will give you the desire for what He calls you to? When may this not be true?

4) Do you think it is appropriate to re-**Altar** one's life from time to time? Why or why not?

Chapter Seventeen

The **Altar'd** Personal and Group Experience

Questions to Get You Started

What if you need more help? I would encourage all of you, and especially the small groups who are going through this book, to go through these steps slowly and thoroughly, together. What if you spent a couple of months wrestling with these questions? Who knows what God could do?

Perhaps this describes some of you: "I really do want to serve Him, but I just don't know what He wants me to do." The following questions may help guide you.

- What bothers you in the church? What bothers you in life? What is something that seems to keep coming up in your life that you wish could be different in your church, in your community, or in your world? You may or may not be able to fix the whole world, but you can impact someone's world. Don't be afraid to dream. Some of these things that

207

keep coming up, that really bother you, very likely could be a passion point for how God would like to use you. Spend some time meditating on what this may be. Bring it before God. What is a practical way God could use you to serve in this way, whether voluntarily or vocationally? Ask God to help you in this. Ask other people for their ideas. Continue to pursue God in this area and wait on Him.

- Who are two godly people who know you well and have seen you in a role or two? Sit down with these people and ask them what they see in you. Ask them for any ideas they may have for how you can be used. Run by them your passions, desires, and the kinds of things that stir you up or bother you. This will do a couple of things. One, God may use them to speak life and direction into you. Two, they may even help you network for the next area in which you can be used by God.

- What are your spiritual gifs? Have you ever done a spiritual gift assessment? Perhaps it is time to do an assessment. You may even want to do it again if it has been awhile. I have found spiritual gift assessments to be remarkably accurate. There are many good ones online and I have found the results over the years to be similar no matter which test I used.

- Try something! Make it your goal to get involved in your church or in a ministry trying out things that you may not be sure of, but could be areas of service which may interest you. Sometimes you just won't be certain until you try. Don't be a bench-warming Christian. Jesus gave His life for you; give back to Him by serving at your church or in a ministry. Come armed with your spiritual gifts and some ideas you may have for service that seem interesting to you.

Altar'd Personal and Group Experience

Does your group want to set up a special experience to take time before God to seek His will and offer your lives to Him? Perhaps you want to hike to a special place together and then spend time on your knees before God offering your lives to Him. Perhaps someone has an idea that would make this experience more memorable. Maybe you could do a weekend retreat together to seek God collectively and individually in order to help one another discover, to a greater degree, how God may want to use you.

Perhaps some of you really want to serve God, but you just don't know what He wants from you yet. If you follow through on processing these things together, this could become a very valuable time in your lives. If you agree to this process, please give permission for the leader to hold you accountable to completing the process. Even if you spent just a couple of months wrestling with these questions, both individually and collectively, it would be time well spent. Who knows what God can do as you seek Him together? It would be good to devote a notebook to this process and write down what God brings to your mind.

The Summary Chapter

Altar'd at Once

This chapter is written to offer the message of this book in a concise manner. This serves as an overall summary of what the book has to offer. By the end of this chapter a person will have risen to the summit of **Altar'd**. However, from that vantage point, the details—and indeed, some of the very evidence that this book brings to light—will not be fully witnessed.

I happen to be a golfer, and the pinnacle of our sport is the Masters Golf Tournament at Augusta National Golf Club in Augusta, Georgia. Every April, millions of people enjoy the beauty of the Augusta grounds from their television sets. A couple of years ago, with a Chevy, tent, and a lack of tickets, my daughter and I drove from Wisconsin to Augusta, hoping to get in. I even wrote the chairman looking for tickets, to no avail. Amazingly, we were blessed to get in and enjoy the event for three days! After watching on TV for so many years, we were compelled to take the full journey and see it for ourselves. No matter how much a person has been told about the perfection of the landscape and grass, one cannot fully appreciate it until they see it for themselves. My daughter, who was twelve at the time, upon entry, knelt down, pointed to the ground, and said, "Dad, is this grass?" She thought it might have been artificial turf.

I hope by reading this summary chapter, **Altar'd** at Once, you are compelled to take the full journey in order to experience the entire message for yourself. If not, at least I hope you enjoy it on TV!

One of the most difficult aspects of communicating the message and evidence for Christianity is sharing the bad news. Yet the bad news is critical in helping people appreciate and accept the good news. The message of the Bible could, in some ways, be compared to a patient going to a doctor who receives the extremely discouraging news that cancer has been discovered, which, if left unattended, will result in the loss of life. However, the doctor indicates there are more tests to run and, following the tests, says he would like to meet again. After the testing, the doctor comes in, has a glowing smile, and says, "Further testing has shown that the cancer in you has not spread; it can easily be treated with medicine. You have a wonderful, long life ahead of you!" What a relief! The person's life will be saved!

In Christianity, the bad news is that we all have a disease, and it will eventually kill us if left untreated. Further tests have revealed we all are infected. However, as long as we have breath, there is still time to be cured. There is a solution. Healing medicine exists. What is so incredibly important is that when we understand the diagnosis and then receive and accept the medicine, we can experience an exciting, new, purposeful life.

So then, what is this disease? How did we acquire it? How are we cured? Lastly, if and when we are cured, what would our proper response be to the One who healed us? Answering these questions, with verifiable evidence, and then discovering our proper and purposeful response to the questions, is the message of **Altar'd.** Let's begin.

When God created man, He put him in a garden and gave him the mission to be fruitful and multiply God's image and likeness. At this point in history, God's physical presence was with man in the garden. At this time, there was nothing separating their relationship. God gave man direct verbal instruction to not eat of a particular tree in the garden. Unfortunately, the devil used one of his very best tactics—one he still uses today. He got man to doubt God and God's Word. As a result, Adam and Eve ate from that forbidden tree. This was the first sin of mankind. Adam and Eve, when they fell into sin, then did what is still so very common among people today. They literally *hid from God* in the garden. Today, when people sin and don't fully comprehend the cure, they very well may hide from God by not seeking Him, by not reading his Word, and they may discontinue attending church. This only continues to exacerbate the problem, and generally it leads to increased sin and separation from God. This sin separated Adam and Eve from a holy God. Adam and Eve had to depart the garden and the direct presence of God. God and sin do not go together. The story of God, from this point in history onward, records and reveals God's desire to draw man near again. Take comfort that God's desire is to be in relationship with man. Even when we fall into sin, He is not without a plan.

After Adam and Eve were banned from the garden they certainly multiplied, but instead of multiplying goodness, they multiplied people infected with the same disease; and all of mankind has been infected with and participated in sin ever since. The human problem is that we all sin and have fallen short of the glory of God (Romans 3:23). This sin, much like a disease, can destroy our lives. A cure exists, but the price of the cure is extremely high. Amazingly, God is willing to pay the price. The question then becomes twofold. Will we accept the cure? And, once we truly understand what God did for us, will our lives reflect our gratefulness to Him?

Down the road in biblical history, God miraculously performs one of the grandest events ever to take place on earth. This special Old Testament happening, as we'll later see fully, shines a bright light on our ultimate cure. This event and how it is later fulfilled is one of the most compelling evidences and important understandings to help one believe in the message of Christianity. This grand event is known as the Passover.

Due to a famine in the land, God's people, the Israelites, are forced to go to Egypt. They go there because God foretold to one of their own brothers (Joseph), who had become a leader in Egypt, that there would be an extended famine, and that Joseph should save grain. When the famine hit with full severity, the only place to buy grain was in Egypt. The Israelites ended up selling all they had to buy grain to survive. When their money ran out, they sold their services in order to be fed. At first, they were treated well, but after hundreds of years new leadership had developed in Egypt, and now the Israelites were treated very poorly, as slaves. From Egypt they cried out for freedom and God heard their cry. The events surrounding their freedom from the Egyptian pharaoh would become known as the Passover. The Passover was the tenth plague, in a series of plagues, designed to change the Egyptian pharaoh's mind to let God's people go free. In this final plague, a spirit of destruction was going to come over Egypt and kill all firstborn cattle and children. Pharaoh himself had a firstborn son, so this was going to hit home. In one infamous night, the 14th day of Nissan on the Hebrew calendar, God gave the Israelites some very important instructions to be saved from this coming destruction.

God told the Israelites to commemorate what was about to take place by sacrificing a lamb and eating it together as families. There were several important instructions given about the lamb. The instructions important for us to remember were that the lamb had to be unblemished, they were not to break any of its bones, and they were to take some blood of the lamb and put it over the doorposts of their homes. When they followed these instructions, God told them, the spirit of destruction would come and "pass over" any home where the blood was atop the doorpost. That night, they followed God's instructions, and indeed, that very night, Pharaoh's firstborn son and cattle died. Pharaoh, who previously would not let God's people go free, finally relented and let them go. God's people, who were instructed to be ready, left immediately. Unfortunately, soon after, Pharaoh changed his mind and chased down the Israelites and trapped them by the Red Sea. This is when God once again did the miraculous. He parted the sea, and the Israelites walked through the walls of water on dry ground. When the Egyptians chased after them, the sea closed in on them and God's people were finally free. This entire episode became known as the Passover. It is the grandest story of the Old Testament. It is the day the blood of lambs saved them, and they became free to worship God. God told them to remember this day forever, through all generations. Every year, on the 14th of Nissan, on that one special day annually, they were instructed to rejoice together through the offering of a lamb and a celebratory meal.

Despite this awesome display of God's power, God's people still had the same problem that has perpetuated since Adam's day. That problem was sin. Even though God continued to do miracles to provide for them in the dessert, including providing water from a rock and bread from the sky, sin continued to rear its ugly head. One time, the Israelite leader at the time, Moses, went away for an extended period of time to gain instruction from God on how to lead this rebellious people. While he was away, thinking Moses may not return, the people decided to make for themselves something to worship. They made an image of a calf out of gold and began to worship it. We all tend to worship something. God's desire is that it would be Him. When Moses came back, he and God were not pleased. Some of the Israelites lost their lives. But then God did something very special, and it has ties to both the Passover and the message of this book. God gave Moses instructions to build a dwelling place, a *tabernacle*, as it would be called. It was a place where the presence of God would be in the camp, among the people. This tabernacle could be described as a fenced-in courtyard with a two-chamber tent in the middle. God would make His presence known to the priests and to the people through a cloud that would hover over the inner tent-like structure, within the courtyard. God's people were instructed to set up camp all the way around this tabernacle in order that they would not forget about Him. This makes a lot of sense. As people, if we do not do something regularly to remember God and place our thoughts on Him, we can become easily complacent and forget about Him and His priorities. When was the last time you followed God's instruction to "be still and know that I am God" (Psalm 46:10, ESV)? Many times people wonder where God is despite the fact they have not been still to read their Bibles, come to church, and seek Him with all their hearts.

God has said, "You will seek me and find me,

when you seek me with all your heart."

(JEREMIAH 29:13, ESV)

So now, with this tabernacle, God had come as near to His people as He had come since the garden. With the tabernacle God made a way for sinful man to be made clean and to draw near to Him again. In order to receive atonement (forgiveness) for sin, they could bring a lamb or goat to the entrance of the tabernacle and sacrifice that animal in honor of God. In order to do so, they would bring their animal, which would need to be an unblemished one, place their hand on the top of its back, and then sacrifice the animal, typically with a knife to the throat. In this way the animal would serve as a means of atonement. The punishment for sin was, in a very real sense, placed on the animal as a substitute. In order for this to be rightly done, the animal had to die, blood had to be shed, and the blood would then be sprinkled on the altar. The animal was then often used as food for the priests, who handled the care of the tabernacle. This may seem extreme to us in the modern world, but it was very common for someone in that day. Today we go to the grocery store to buy our food. However, even my wife's grandma lived on a farm, and they processed their own chickens before putting them on the dinner table. So don't get lost on animal sacrifice. If you eat meat, an animal is being processed. Back then they were used to doing this themselves.

In this way people could be made in right standing with God. The sin that prevented their close relationship with God was now dealt with through the offered sacrifice. However, they were only made right temporarily. As they continued to sin, they would need to offer a sacrifice once again. This would also likely prevent them from sinning because animals were extremely valuable.

So let's crystalize what has been said: All people have inherited the sin of Adam. Sin separates us from God. God used a lamb and the blood of the lamb to save His people at Passover, which became a special holiday taking place on Nissan 14 every year. God came up with a way to draw near, despite our sin, through the tabernacle. Man could be forgiven of his sin by offering a lamb at its gate. God's rules were that the lamb needed to be unblemished and that blood would need to be shed.

We now need to take a brief respite from the story of God to bring to light an amazing recent discovery. This discovery is known as the Dead Sea Scrolls. The Dead Sea Scrolls, to keep it simple, are copies of the Old Testament. They are called the Dead Sea Scrolls because they were discovered in caves in the Dead Sea area, in

Israel, in the Middle East. The Old Testament is the large portion of the Bible containing all the events before the time of Jesus. What makes the Dead Sea Scrolls so important is their age. The Dead Sea Scrolls are the oldest copies of the Old Testament in existence. Prior to the Dead Sea Scrolls we did not have any copies of the Old Testament that were older than the events of the New Testament (after Jesus). We always believed, for many reasons, that the Old Testament was written and recorded prior to Jesus, but we did not have copies that predated Him. After all, Jesus died, many believe (and as I will argue), in 33 A.D., so any scroll older than Jesus would be more than 2,000 years old. It's hard to get a document to last that long, especially in that day. As it turns out, a group of people, who were likely facing persecution, hid these scrolls in caves, and they had been stored in this library cavern since 300 B.C.! They were not discovered until the late 1940s. It is truly one of the most amazing discoveries. These copies of the Bible are important because they prove without a shadow of doubt that anything written in the Old Testament was indeed written before Jesus ever walked the earth. In the Old Testament, many things were written about the coming of Jesus and what would happen to Him. Now that it is proven that the Old Testament predates Him, we can acquire an abundance of faith by observing how accurately the Old Testament predicted the events of His birth, life, and death.

In the full portion of this book, **Altar'd,** the Old Testament prophecies about Jesus are written about in detail and their fulfillment in His life is shown. In summary, here are some of the things the Old Testament said would happen: they foretold that Jesus would be born of a virgin (Isaiah 7:14), come from the family line of David (Isaiah 9:6, 7), and that He would be born in the city of Bethlehem (Micah 5:2-4). Keep in mind that most of these prophecies were written five hundred to seven hundred years before they occurred. The story of Jesus' birth, and how God fulfilled these predictions, is quite remarkable.

We shall now turn to the fulfillments, in the New Testament, which grow in magnitude from His birth to His death. First off, the New Testament indicates that Jesus was born to Mary, a virgin, who was impregnated by the Holy Spirit (Luke 1:26-38); and the lineage of Jesus' parents also is recorded, illustrating that He indeed came from the family line of David (Matthew 1:1-6), just as foretold. In addition, God had directed the events of the day to get Joseph and Mary to Bethlehem so that when the time came for Jesus to be born, they would be there (Luke 2:1-7). Mary and Joseph, Jesus' parents, were not even living near Bethlehem. What happened is the king of the land determined a census must be taken, and each family was ordered to go to its native town to register. Since Joseph, and Jesus' family line, both came from David, whose hometown was Bethlehem, they were required to go to Bethlehem to register. It is quite remarkable that at the right time, Mary delivered, while they were in Bethlehem. I'm pretty sure this was before medicine was developed to induce childbirth! No worries; God has his own. In this way God fulfilled that Jesus would be born in Bethlehem, just as He indicated would happen five hundred years earlier through Micah. There is even great evidence regarding the special star that indicated to the wise men that a king had been born. Due to technology, we now know the location of the stars and planets at any time in history, both in the past and in the future, because stars and planets move precisely, like clockwork. In the year of Jesus' suspected birth, the two brightest-looking "stars" in the sky, which were actually the planets Jupiter and Venus, came so close together, from our vantage point on Earth, that they looked like one massive, bright star. This event is actually on display at several planetariums and is generally noted as producing one of the brightest-looking would-be stars (planets) ever to shine in the sky.

God fulfilled the virgin birth, this birth city, and brought His child to earth in the family line (David) that He said He would. Although I love to see how God worked out all of these events for Jesus' birth, it is in Jesus' death that we see still more miraculous evidence that can be further tested. We'll now turn to these events.

In the Old Testament it was said that Jesus would be despised and rejected by men (Isaiah 53:3); that He would be pierced for our transgressions (Isaiah 53:5); that with His wounds we would be healed (Isaiah 53:5); and that on Him was laid the iniquity of us all (Isaiah 53:6). In addition, it was said that when He was afflicted He would not open His mouth in defense (Isaiah 53:7); that He would be like a lamb led to the slaughter (Isaiah 53:7); that His grave would be made with the wicked and also with the rich in His death (Isaiah 53:9); and that He would bear the sin of many (Isaiah 53:12). Without being redundant, it is important to note that all of these references are from seven hundred years before His life, and the predating of these words has been made crystal clear by the Dead Sea Scrolls!

In the Old Testament, we have recorded what is known as the Old Covenant with God. A covenant is an agreement made by God with His people. There are several in the Old Testament. Some are unilateral, made by God alone, and some are bilateral, meaning the Israelites confirmed their agreement to them. In the Old Testament, when God would make a covenant with His people, it would be ratified with an offering and sealed with blood. In this same Old Testament it was foretold through the prophet Jeremiah that one day God would usher in a New Covenant (a new agreement) in which God would forgive our inequities and remember our sins no more (Jeremiah 31:34). How does that sound? Sounds pretty good to me! All of these prophecies set the stage for the life and death of Jesus.

There are so many other prophecies I am leaving out for the purpose of getting you to the main point. The last one, which is very important to illustrate, comes from the prophet Joel. This Old

Testament prophet foretold that when the coming of "the day of the Lord" arrived, the Spirit of God would be poured out, the sun would be turned to darkness, and the moon be turned to blood (Joel 2:28-32). Also beautifully recorded in that passage is the statement that, "And it shall come to pass that everyone who calls on the name of the Lord shall be saved."

All of these things just noted, when you add them up, record with tremendous detail specifics about what would happen at the death of Jesus, and what would be accomplished with His death. Some of the prophecies even tell us that the sun and moon would announce His sacrifice. If all of these things did indeed come to pass, exactly as foretold, five hundred to seven hundred years earlier through the prophets, one must admit it would be astonishing. How could it happen unless God orchestrated all of this as a grand conductor?

Many could read the following passage about the last days of Jesus' life and, as a result of not understanding the Old Testament, miss out on the in-depth meaning.

> ...the disciples came to Jesus saying, "Where will you have us
> prepare for you to eat the Passover?" He said, "Go into the city to a
> certain man and say to him, 'The Teacher says, My time is at hand.
> I will keep the Passover at your house with my disciples.'"
> And the disciples did as Jesus directed them,
> and they prepared the Passover.
>
> (MATTHEW 26:17a-19, ESV)

We need to pause for a moment to gather some information that will help us be able to take in all that will soon happen and be fulfilled. First off, the day of the week recorded above is a Thursday. Although our day changes from one to the next at midnight, that is not how a day changed for the Jewish people at that time. For them, the next day started at sunset. So when the sun went down on Thursday, it became a Friday. So on that Thursday, during the day, they went to prepare for the Passover meal. We have already learned that the Passover is one of the most special days for a Jewish person in the entire year. They were instructed by God to remember and commemorate that day with a celebratory meal, every year, on the 14th day of Nissan. At sunset, when they would be enjoying the meal together, it would be Passover Friday. Jesus, being Jewish, and His disciples, were doing just as they should, honoring God by remembering the Passover. This is very significant, as we shall see.

At this particular Passover meal, Jesus did some very special things with His disciples. Jesus washed their feet; he watched as Judas (one of the twelve apostles) left to betray Him; and Jesus introduced what has now become a new celebration; we memorialize it as the Last Supper. On this evening Jesus took bread and wine, which are typical of a normal Passover meal, and conveyed new meaning in them.

Now as they were eating, Jesus took bread,
and after blessing it broke it and gave it to the disciples, and said,
"Take, eat, this is my body."
And he took a cup, and when he had given thanks
he gave it to them, saying,
"Drink of it, all of you, <u>for this is my blood of the covenant,</u>
<u>which is poured out for many for the forgiveness of sins.</u>
I tell you I will not drink again of this fruit of the vine
until that day when I drink it new
with you in my Father's kingdom."

(MATTHEW 26:26-29, ESV)

From this Passover, which we also remember now as the Last Supper, we received what is now known as the Eucharist, or Communion. There are many things we need to glean from this. Jesus takes a cup symbolizing His blood and says that this is the blood of the covenant that is poured out for many for the forgiveness of sins. Do you recall how a covenant was sealed and ratified in the Old Testament? It was done so with both an offering and with blood. I would also like us to recall what Jeremiah prophesied about the coming of a New Covenant. Jeremiah said—a full seven hundred years earlier—that in this New Covenant God would forgive our sins and remember them no more (Jeremiah 31:34). So Jesus, on this night, at the Passover, takes the cup, representing His blood, and says: This is the blood of the covenant which is poured out for many for the forgiveness of sins.

It is all beginning to come together.

In the middle of that night Jesus is arrested as Judas led the authorities to where they could find Him. On this Friday, Good Friday, which is still Passover, we will see how much of what God foretold comes true. When Jesus was arrested and questioned, He did not defend Himself (John 19:9), just as the prophet Isaiah earlier said. Jesus knew his blood would be shed. He came to die for us all. So why defend yourself when your purpose is to die? After being questioned and beaten by many, Jesus was hung on a cross. What is so interesting and powerful are the specific events of His death. When Jesus was put on a cross, two thieves were also killed with Him. One on His right and one on His left. You may recall earlier it was predicted by Isaiah that Jesus would be assigned a grave with the wicked and with the rich in His death. Two thieves were killed with Jesus. This fulfills the portion about "the wicked" in that prophecy. Jesus was put on the cross at about noon (John 19:14). At this same time, as was represented by witnesses on the scene that day, the sun was darkened—an extremely rare occurrence (Luke 23:44). We don't know how this occurred, but many ancient sources also confirm the sun was darkened that day. In fact, even in the Olympics, right around that same time, there are written records that state a "failure of the sun" took place. The Old Testament prophet Joel prophesied hundreds of years earlier, as previously shared, that this is exactly what would take place. How does all of this happen unless God made it happen?

It is now getting late in the day, the Friday of Passover, and at sunset the day would flip to a Saturday. Saturday was a Sabbath, a day of rest described in the Bible as being reserved for the seventh day. So the authorities wanted the three men on the cross killed, and their bodies off the cross, before sunset. Let's read about some remarkable things that now take place.

> **So the soldiers came and broke the legs of the first, and of the**
> **other who had been crucified with him. But when they came to**
> **Jesus and saw that he was already dead, they did not break his legs.**
> **But one of the soldiers pierced his side with a spear**
> **and at once there came out blood and water.**
>
> (JOHN 19:32-34, ESV)

The specificity of this, as we will see, is truly remarkable. They see that Jesus is dead, and they want to ensure the quick and certain death of all three men, so they go to the thieves and break their legs. Their legs would be used to hold them up on their crosses, and without the strength of their legs they would soon die of asphyxiation. However, when they get to Jesus, and see that He is dead, they don't break His legs. Rather, to ensure He is dead, they pierce Him in the side with a spear and His blood comes pouring out. Remarkable.

I believe this is the first of several special and powerful forms of evidence. The day is Passover. Do you recall the instructions for the Passover lamb of the Old Testament? The lamb used was to be unblemished, its bones were not to be broken, and the blood was to be used as a symbol over the doorposts to save the Israelites. God, nearly two thousand years after the first Passover, on this Passover, has His Son die on a cross as the Lamb of God who takes away the sins of the world. His Son was blameless. And to make sure we would see that this is God's Lamb, His bones were not broken. Think about it. The legs of the two thieves were both broken; only Jesus' bones were not broken. And to see how God continues to fulfill His word, we carry on. Do you recall what Isaiah prophesied with the help of God approximately seven hundred years earlier?

But he was pierced for our transgressions,

he was crushed for our inequities,

upon him was the chastisement that brought us peace,

and with his wounds we are healed.

All we like sheep have gone astray,

we have turned—every one—to his own way;

and the Lord laid on him the iniquity of us all.

(ISAIAH 53:5, 6, ESV)

Neither thief was pierced, but just as was foretold, Jesus was pierced. Bringing it together, then, God has always had in mind a means for restoring His relationship with sinful man. His means has always been through an offering. God saved people on the first Passover through the sacrifice of a lamb and its blood. In the desert God forgave His people through an offering brought to the tabernacle. Now, on God's special day, Passover, Jesus offers His life and sheds His blood to show us clearly that He is the Lamb of God who takes away the sins of the world (John 1:29). Of all the days that Jesus could have died, He died on this one special day. Do you realize the statistical probability of this? One day out of 365 days is, statistically, a probability of only .27 percent. That is less than one-third of 1 percent chance that Jesus would die on that day! He could have died on any other of the 364 days, but God had Him die on that one special day to show you and me that He knows what He is doing and that Jesus is God's offering for sin. Jesus is the Lamb of God who takes away the sins of the world!

All of us have sinned, and that sin separates us from a relationship with God. God desires to forgive us and restore us to relationship with Him. His means of forgiveness is through sacrifice. No longer can we, or do we, bring animals to God to be offered. No one brings a lamb to church. Even if we did, it would not work. Jesus is the once-and-for-all, final Lamb of God, and when we trust in Him as Lord and Savior we receive forgiveness of sins, the Holy Spirit, and a renewed relationship with God now and forever.

We are now able to make sense of one of the most popular verses in the Bible. It is so well known for a very good reason.

> **For God so loved the world**
> **that he gave his only son,**
> **that whoever believes in him**
> **should not perish but have eternal life.**
>
> (JOHN 3:16, ESV)

Whoever truly believes in Jesus has eternal life! God gave His Son for that to occur, and God did it because of His great love for us. As great as that verse is, it should not be read in isolation. As well known as that verse is, one gets a more complete picture with the next two verses.

> **For God did not send his Son into the world**
> **to condemn the world, but in order that**
> **the world might be saved through him.**
>
> (JOHN 3:17, ESV)

This shows that God, in sending His Son to die for us, did so not to condemn people, but rather to save people. God's desire is for people to be saved through His Son. That comes through true faith, and true faith is required. The next verse is very important, and it also helps shed light on the message of this book.

Whoever believes in him is not condemned,
but whoever does not believe is condemned already,
because he has not believed
in the name of the only Son of God.

(JOHN 3:18, ESV)

This verse illustrates something everyone must know. It is critical for us to know, and also for all whom we love. Our default position is condemnation and separation...but it does not have to stay that way. Why is this true? The answer to this question shapes both our lives and our very purpose. The answer is: because of the fact we are all sinners, and sin separates us from God, we all need a solution. God provided our substitute. God provided the solution. God followed His Old Testament rules and patterns, all to provide us with forgiveness. God provided the ultimate offering. God provided the Lamb of God who takes away the sins of the world. God had His Son shed blood.

So then, does God just overlook sin? No, actually God declared a punishment for sin. Because God is just, someone has to pay for our sins. A just God follows through, just like a just judge delivers a penalty for a lawbreaker. God follows His own justice, but He does so in one of the most loving, sacrificial, amazing ways possible. He takes out our wrongs on His Son! God did it because it was necessary, as He followed His own rules for providing forgiveness, and He wanted to be in relationship with us. To do so He paid the cost of forgiveness. The medicine for our healing exists—but we still have to make a choice.

We have to choose to take the medicine. We need a cure for our sin, and God provided the cure in His Son's death. In order to receive forgiveness we need to receive Jesus through faith. We all have a choice. Here it is, very clearly and directly. We can pay for our sin ourselves, in Hell forever, or we can place our faith in Jesus as our Lord and Savior and our sin gets placed upon Him on that cross. When we, in faith, believe this, we are forgiven and now receive the proper motivation to live our lives in gratitude to the One who first gave His. Some may feel the reference to Hell (or Heaven) is a harsh one. Can't we just be nice and not be so harsh? Imagine for a moment a child is running across the road for a ball with an oncoming car approaching. What would any good mother, father, or really, any person do? They would scream, "Stop!" Would that scream be harsh, or love? Clearly love, right? Why would we want anyone to be harmed? No, the Bible gives us warnings because God loves us so much He wants us to know the consequences for our sin so we won't stay in them. Rather, His desire is that we know the truth and the truth would set us free. Actually, the saddest thing of all would be for someone to be misinformed, and as a result not receive forgiveness, purpose, and the eternal life offered by God. Can you imagine someone paying for the consequences of their unforgiven sin in Hell and having the ability to look up to us who were forgiven, and were in Heaven, and ask us, "Why didn't you tell me so I too could have been forgiven?" References to salvation and condemnation are clear throughout the Bible. It is love that shares both, so that no one has to be condemned, and so that we are all motivated to be saved and to share His saving message.

Let me offer one last question before we move on to what it means to be **Altar'd**. If we would have been OK in our sin, and if we did not need a sacrifice, then why would God have His Son crucified? It was necessary because we needed an offering. God lovingly and willingly made it. To God be the glory.

What happens next is truly incredible. Jesus rises from the dead! I go over this at length in the book. I will do so here in brief.

Jesus comes back to show Himself over and over again to convince His disciples that He had the power to rise again. After all, who comes back from the dead like He did? And not only so, but then to come back and be able to show the marks on His hands, feet, and the pierce mark on His side? Not only does Jesus come back and show Himself again and again and again to His disciples, He also shows Himself to many others. The Bible records that Jesus showed Himself to more than five hundred people!

Many of you remember the 1995 trial of O.J. Simpson; he was charged with the murder of his ex-wife and another man. Many, many people believe Simpson was guilty of the murders. Yet, on the criminal aspect of that trial, he was found not guilty. One of the most memorable statements of the trial was: "If the gloves don't fit, you must acquit." (It was made by a Simpson defense attorney.) Above all else, why do you think O.J. Simpson got off? When I ask this question, many responses that are given include that he had good lawyers. Or that his fame helped him. Or perhaps that it was the gloves that were reportedly used seemed to be too small for his hands. I have three children and many times I have squeezed into a pair of gloves because mine were not easily accessible. Although these are all intelligent answers, there is a far more compelling reason O.J. got off.

No one saw him do it.

There were no eyewitnesses to the murder. If one person would have saw Simpson do it, he probably would have been found guilty. Attorneys, of course, would have tried everything they could to discredit that witness. But what if five, or even ten, people saw him murder his ex-wife? He would have been toast! Friends, Jesus died and rose from the dead, His apostles and five hundred others saw Him alive again, some of them on multiple occasions. The evidence for Jesus' resurrection is strong and solid. Some may wonder if the disciples fabricated His resurrection. If that were true, what would have been their motive? They did not have a printing press to sell books. We never hear any evidence that they profited in any way. There are even other nonbiblical sources, like the writer Josephus, who record that Jesus was noted as rising again. Josephus was not even a believer of Jesus. Jesus' resurrection really comes down to whether the disciples were telling the truth or lying. If you read it for yourself, I think you will be convinced they are telling the truth. Even more convincing, however, is what happened to them as the rest of their lives played out. Nearly every one of the twelve apostles of Christ was martyred for his faith. They were willing to die for what they believed. If they were lying, why would they die for a lie? I mean, if they made it up, they would know they were making it up, and if they could have saved their lives by telling the truth, they would have. Why would they not deny this so-called resurrection and live? Yet the records indicate they were killed for their faith. They could not deny what they saw with their own eyes. Jesus indeed rose from the dead. He is risen indeed!

There is one more piece of evidence that is truly astounding; I'd like to share it now. In the full book I go into detail as to the exact day that many believe Jesus died. It is actually very possible to come up with an exact date from the detail recorded in the Bible. As an example, we know that Jesus died on a Friday and that it was Passover. Since Passover is only one day per year, one can take a look when the Passovers would have landed on Fridays around that period of history. When that is done, there are two to three decent options, but one shines forth. The best date, with evidence I will now illustrate, is Friday, April 3, 33 A.D. In order to share the evidence, we need to move down the path from Jesus' death on a cross to another Jewish holiday known as Pentecost. *Pente* can be translated "fifty." Pentecost comes fifty days after Passover. Pentecost is a Jewish religious day in which the Jews celebrate the first grain harvest of the year. When Jesus ascended to Heaven, about forty days after His death, He told His disciples to wait in

Jerusalem for the Holy Spirit, which would soon come. The day the Holy Spirit came to all whom believed in Him was Pentecost. Isn't it cool how God works? He ties together Old Testament special days, which He prescribed, with grand New Testament fulfillment. How does this stuff happen unless God makes it happen? Just as Jesus died on Passover, his Spirit came on Pentecost. The day His Spirit came was quite astounding. All the people could tell something special happened to the believers of Jesus. The people around Jerusalem that day thought these new Christian people were acting strangely—possibly even drunk—as they were talking in foreign tongues. This is when Peter assumes his leadership position and gives a powerful message to all the people surrounding him in Jerusalem that day. To read this speech for yourself, just turn to Acts chapter 2. One of the things Peter does, in justifying what they perceived as strange behavior, was to take them back to the prophet Joel, referenced earlier. Peter quotes Joel:

> **"And in the last days it shall be, God declares,**
>
> **that I will pour out my Spirit on all flesh,**
>
> **and your sons and your daughters shall prophesy, and your young**
>
> **men shall see visions, and your old men shall dream dreams; even**
>
> **on my male servants and female servants in those days I will pour**
>
> **out my Spirit, and they shall prophesy. And I will show wonders in**
>
> **heavens above and signs on the earth below, blood, and fire, and**
>
> **vapor of smoke; the sun shall be turned to darkness**
>
> **and the moon to blood, before the day the Lord comes,**
>
> **the great and magnificent day. And it shall come to pass that**
>
> **everyone who calls upon the name of the Lord shall be saved."**

(ACTS 2:17-21, QUOTING JOEL 2:28-32, BOTH ESV)

Peter then goes on to tell them:

"Men of Israel, hear these words; Jesus of Nazareth, a man attested

to you by God with mighty works and wonders and signs that God
did through him in your midst as you yourselves know–..."

(ACTS 2:22, ESV)

Peter is reminding them and saying: "Don't be surprised by
what you are now seeing in these people; this is given them
through the Spirit." Joel said it would come, and look at all the
other *mighty works, wonders, and signs that God did through
Him in your midst as you yourselves know.* So besides the fact
that people are speaking in foreign tongues, by the aid of the
Spirit, what else could Peter be referring to that the people
would be able to identify with, that they had already seen for
themselves? The two most profound would be that, just as
Joel prophesied, the sun was darkened and the moon turned
to blood. We have already seen that at Jesus' death the sun
was darkened. This alone would be incredible for the people
to have witnessed. After all, the sun being darkened during the
day would be an incredibly rare and attention-getting occurrence. The fact that this happened at the death of Jesus, as God
said it would, is even more amazing. But there is more. What
about this moon turning to blood? Could Peter be saying, "Hey,
you have seen the blood moon, another prophecy that Joel said
would happen? Since you have seen both the sun darkened and
the moon turned to blood, don't doubt, but believe." Now remember the result of Peter's message. When Peter gets done
sharing his message, thousands of people confess their faith
through baptism. So something Peter says, and the evidence
that is gleaned from it, helps convince the people that what he
is saying must be true. Could the blood moon have something
to do with it?

What is a blood moon? A blood moon is what is known as a
lunar eclipse. A lunar eclipse is a rare occurrence. It takes place,
on average, in any given region, only about once a year. A lunar

eclipse occurs when the earth, during its orbit, comes between the sun and the moon, and therefore the moon is in the shadow of the earth. When the moon is in that shadow, it looks blood red. That is why it is called a blood moon.

As we have learned with modern technology, we can go back in time and put the stars, planets, sun, and moon in the sky exactly in the positions they were on any day, including *that day*, with precision. So if we go back to April 3, 33 A.D., what we will find? In order to do this research, we will gain some assistance from astronomers at the national space agency, NASA. NASA should be a pretty good source for this kind of thing. It is truly incredible to see what we can now see for ourselves. On April 3, 33 A.D., at 5:38 p.m., as could be seen from Jerusalem, a lunar eclipse occurred. Check it out for yourself at these NASA website links.

http://eclipse.gsfc.nasa.gov/5MCLEmap/0001-0100/LE0033-04-03P.gif

http://eclipse.gsfc.nasa.gov/JLEX/JLEX-AS.html

This is truly amazing. The Bible says that God counts the stars and knows them by name. That always seemed so expansive to me—until I saw this evidence. Can you even imagine how amazing this is? God, on the day of His Son's death, has the sun, earth, and moon all lined up, on that one special day, Passover, to form a rare lunar eclipse, thereby fulfilling the words of His Old Testament prophet Joel, spoken about five hundred years earlier. Only God can do that! And since He can do that, and since He can come off that cross and show Himself alive again, and since He did it out of His great love to forgive us of our sins, He is worthy of our all.

You have now taken in the evidence. These very things are what make me convinced to offer my life to serve His Kingdom. That is His desire for all of us. So how do we make this personal for ourselves? How is it that we receive forgiveness and the gift of eternal life? The Bible says:

>...because, if you confess with your mouth
>
>**Jesus is Lord**
>
>**and believe in your heart**
>
>**that God raised him from the dead,**
>
>**you will be saved.**
>
>**For with the heart one believes and is justified,**
>
>**and with the mouth one confesses and is saved.**
>
>(ROMANS 10:9, 10, ESV)

So one must confess Jesus is Lord and believe that God raised Him from the dead. This becomes deeper when one digs in. Many people want a Savior, but few are willing to make Him Lord. To confess Jesus as Lord is to be willing to make Him master. To be willing, out of faith, to say, "Jesus, I want to follow you. I don't merely want forgiveness, but I want your help in living a life that is about pleasing you."

After all, if Jesus is master, then we are His servants. What good is a servant to a master if the servant doesn't want to serve? With that being said, we would fail on our own strength. We need His help to be a good servant. When we surrender to God, in faith, we receive the Holy Spirit. The same Spirit God gave at Pentecost. The Holy Spirit helps us, strengthens us, gives us spiritual gifts, and empowers us to serve God. Believe in Jesus. Surrender to Jesus. Let Him know you believe in Him. Seek His help in becoming a better follower. Why not do this now? Consider this prayer to begin a new life in Christ. This is what it means to become born again. To have a new life in Christ, to get to start over, with the help of His Spirit.

God,

I have come to realize that I am a sinner
and that my sin keeps me from You now and forever.
I now understand that in Your great love
you sent Your son, Jesus, to be the final Lamb of God
who takes away the sins of the world.
I believe in Jesus
and I willingly receive Him as the Lord of my life.
I believe You conquered sin by rising from the dead.
Thank You for sending Him to forgive me.
Please fill me with Your Holy Spirit,
and help me to live a life
that is pleasing to You.
In Jesus' name.

Amen.

After reading this summary chapter, I encourage you to go back to the beginning of this book and take in the entire work. There is so much more covered, including detailed evidence and my personal story of transformation (found in chapter 3). You may even want to see if you can gather some people to read the book together. There are discussion questions for your use. At the very least, I would suggest reading chapters 15-17, as they are not covered in this summary and will flow well directly from where we ended here.

I truly hope God uses this book to help your life and grow His Kingdom. To leave a comment, please go to **Altardthebook.com**.

Jay Cavaiani
JUNE 2015

Small Group Discussion Guide

A note about small groups

It truly would be great to encourage other people to attend a small group to read this book and discuss what they are learning. Chapter 17 gives some guidance on a group or personal exercise that is very much recommended. The book offers a great opportunity to evaluate our lives and discover what God may have in store for our future. Some of the questions included for small groups are there to make sure the reader takes the time to personally mine the evidence recorded in the book. In that way they learn the evidence for themselves. Some of these questions are not so discussion oriented. They are there to help the reader take the time, hopefully prior to coming together, to discern the evidence. Other questions are there to promote discussion on how we can apply what is learned to our lives.

It would be wise for the leader to go over the questions regarding the Biblical evidence to make sure everyone fully understands. Then, after doing so, allow for more input on the questions that promote discussion. In addition, at times, two chapters could be covered in one week. In other weeks, it may be wise to spend more than one week on a chapter. You may go to altardthebook. com to see a small group schedule that was used in a study I led.

Endnotes
· · · · · · · · · · · · · · · ·

1. http://www.nytimes.com/1999/06/04/arts/painting-packs-a-million-dollar-surprise.html.

2. *Handbook of Meat Inspection, 3ʳᵈ Edition*, Robert von Ostertag (William R. Jenkins Co. Publishers, 1912), 10.

3. Dictionary.com: Mosaic Covenant definition.

4. http://chronicle.com/blogs/linguafranca/2013/10/21/dude/.

5. http://www.christiananswers.net/q-abr/abr-a023.html.

6. https://bible.org/article/dead-sea-scrolls.

7. http://www.deadseascrolls.org.il/learn-about-the-scrolls/discovery-and-publication?locale=en_US.

8. http://www.ncregister.com/blog/jimmy-akin/jesus-birth-and-when-herod-the-great-really-died.

9. Bethlehem Star video and website: http://www.bethlehemstar.net/.

10. www.askelm.com/star/star001.htm .

11. www.bogan.ca/astro/occultations/2bcocclt.htm.

12. www.bethlehemstar.net/starry-dance/westward-leading, pg 88.

13. www.pewforum.org/2012/12/18/global-religous-landscape-exec/.

14. Cited from: www.creation.mobi/darkness-at-the-crucifixion-metaphor-or-real-history.

15. Maier, Paul. *Pontius Pilate* (Wheaton, Ill.: Tyndale House, 1968), 366. Phlegon's citation is a fragment from Olympiades he Chronika 13, ed. Otto Keller, Rerum Naturalium Scriptores Graeci Minores, 1 (Leipzig Teurber, 1877), 101.

16.   I am indebted to the Bethlehem Star video and website, which first revealed to me this blood moon and the biblical evidence regarding it. Bethlehem Star video and website: http://www.bethlehemstar.net.

Altar'd

**FAITH-BUILDING EVIDENCE
LEADING TO NEW LIFE**